# Contents

# How to Protect Yourself from Killer Computers:

## From the Post Office Scandal to Artificial Intelligence

Junade Ali PhD CEng FIET

Written by Dr Junade Ali
Edited by Christie Moreton
Cover design by Katarina Naskovski

ISBN: 978-1-0686057-1-0

# Introduction

On the 16th of March 2004, Juanita Grossman, a 77-year-old great-grandmother from Indiana, USA, was driving to pick up some medicines from a pharmacy when her 2003 Toyota Camry shot across the road, crashing into a jewellery store.

Her son, Bill, said of the crash: "It was like a car on a slingshot. She was slung across the street into that building."

Grossman was in and out of consciousness for six days following the crash, before dying from her injuries.

The story, however, has a twist.

Grossman was found with both feet jammed down on the brake pedal. On her deathbed, she recounted how she braked furiously but could not slow the car. The *LA Times* reported her son Bill saying, "She kept emphatically saying that the accelerator stuck on her."

It was as if the car had taken on a mind of its own and decided to accelerate, ignoring any instruction to brake.

In another case, on the 10th of June 2006 in Minnesota, USA, Koua Fong Lee was driving his pregnant wife and children home from church in his 1996 Toyota Camry. As he went to exit the freeway, his car accelerated to an estimated 90 miles per hour, crashing into another vehicle and killing all the occupants.

Lee said he'd tried to push the brakes, but nothing happened. A Minnesota jury concluded he must have hit the accelerator instead of the brakes and sentenced him to eight years imprisonment.

After serving almost three years in jail and with evidence collected by the Innocence Project Clinic at the University of Minnesota Law School indicating that the fault actually rested with the engineering of the vehicle, Lee applied for a retrial.

According to ABC News, prosecutors offered him a deal whereby he would be immediately released if he did not challenge his status as a convicted felon. Lee refused to take the deal, and judge Joanne Smith ordered that he be freed, pending a new trial. Less than an hour later, prosecutors announced they would not retry to convict Lee.

Later, Lee took Toyota to court with a theory of how a faulty vehicle could have resulted in the deaths. Toyota attempted to counter the theory with the testimony of a Japanese engineer who claimed there were "robust protocols" for reliability testing, which included days-long heat testing at 280 degrees (presumably Fahrenheit), according to a report by Safety Research & Strategies, Inc. However, shortly before the trial, Toyota filed a declaration from the engineer stating that the company actually did no such testing.

The jury ultimately found Toyota was 60% responsible for the crash that had killed three people and severely injured two.

These are far from the only cases. According to CBS News, the US National Highway

Traffic Safety Administration (NHTSA) alleged that unintended acceleration problems in Toyota vehicles may have killed 89 people and resulted in 57 injuries, according to complaint reports sent to them.

However, a 2019 report in *Capitol Weekly* states that, "Without admitting liability, Toyota since 2014 has settled 537 claims blaming sudden acceleration for crashes that killed or seriously injured people, according to a court document Toyota filed" in September 2019.

Nevertheless, in the case of Bookout v. Toyota, questions turned to the computer systems in the car, and we began to learn more about what was happening.

In 2007, Jean Bookout was driving her 2005 Toyota Camry on an interstate highway in Oklahoma, USA. Her friend, Barbara Schwarz, was in the passenger seat. As Jean went to exit the highway, she realised that she could not stop the car.

In desperation, Jean pulled the parking brake to attempt to stop the car, leaving long skid marks on the road. The car didn't decelerate until it came to a rest with its nose in an embankment. Jean spent two months recovering from head and back injuries. Her friend, Barbara, died in the crash.

Toyota initially recalled the floor mats and then accelerator pedals. However, this issue was not caused by mechanical issues or driver error, as some had attributed responsibility to.

As attention turned to the car's electrical systems, NHTSA needed help to conduct an investigation. As described by *Washington Post* writers Peter Whoriskey and Frank Ahrens, NHTSA had no software engineers or electrical engineers on their staff at the time of the investigation. This appears to be why the NHTSA turned to NASA, the US space agency, to help support their investigation.

Their report was released on the 8th of February 2011 and stated that they were unable to find any computer issues, placing the blame on "sticking" accelerator pedals and accelerator pedals being trapped under floor mats. Whilst NASA did not rule out the issues could have emerged from computer software, their report claimed that: "Our conclusion is Toyota's problems were mechanical, not electrical."

This was despite the fact that on the 4th of February 2010, Toyota themselves had attributed issues in the braking system of one of their models to a software glitch in some Toyota Prius vehicles. Reuters reported that 133,000 Prius vehicles in the US and 52,000 in Europe were to receive the software update.

It would later emerge that NASA hadn't necessarily been able to fully understand the vehicle's computer systems and that there were a number of bugs they weren't aware of.

Bookout launched legal proceedings against Toyota. The Barr Group began investigating Toyota's software, with Michael Barr testifying during the trial. According to the Barr Group, they could only access the computer code in a specially built secure room in Maryland, USA with no internet or phones and a guard station, amongst other security measures.

Barr testified that he found bugs in the code, including ones that could cause unintended acceleration.

Barr said that much of the software violated rules set by the Motor Industry Software Reliability Association (MISRA), a British-based not-for-profit consortium that works to produce standards for writing safety-critical software in the C programming language, which was used to code the vehicle's driving system.

Unlike the cars of previous years, Toyota's vehicles no longer used hydraulics or mechanics to control acceleration or braking – these were done by wires and a computer system.

Barr's testimony also alleged that there were defective safety systems in the software. For example, the slides presented during the testimony claimed the "watchdog" system that checked if any of the computer programs (known as tasks) had crashed was "incapable, ever, of detecting death of majority of tasks".

Barr argued that a single change to a binary one or zero number, which could be caused by cosmic rays, could result in unintended acceleration.

On the 24th of October 2013, a jury found that the software systems could cause unintended acceleration and Toyota ultimately settled the case.

In such a scenario, one of the few potential options available to a driver to save themselves would be to turn off the ignition. In 2013, Toyota made changes to their vehicles with a push start/stop button so that either three quick pushes or a continuous push for two seconds would turn off the ignition (previously only a three-second continuous push would work, something Toyota initially defended as a mechanism to stop cars being turned off accidentally).

The kind of computers involved in this case are known as "embedded systems" – small computers which permutate every aspect of our modern lives, from our cars and the hidden sensors embedded in the road to detect traffic conditions, to our watches and TVs.

The role of computer software more generally is broader than this. Aside from software running on our phones and computers, its power extends to critical national infrastructure – from the submarines armed with nuclear warheads patrolling underwater at every hour of every day, to the software powering power plants and water treatment facilities. This is not to mention the role the internet plays in society and the newfound fears of Artificial Intelligence (AI).

As a software engineer and computer scientist, I have played a role in this reprogramming of society. However, many are unaware of the scale of risk computer software attracts. It has played a role in miscarriages of justice, helped enable criminality and even killed.

New technology always attracts risk. We wouldn't have car crashes if the motor vehicle was never invented, but at the same time they would then not be available to emergency services, logistics companies and commuters. However, as new technology emerges, that isn't to say we shouldn't try to mitigate new risks.

Fundamental to the work of an engineer is trying to balance these competing forces of risk and reward to ensure the rewards always outweigh the risk when a new technology is brought to market.

Having researched many case studies of software failures, there are key learnings that engineers and the general public alike should be aware of so that – both as individuals and as a society – we can protect ourselves from becoming victims to such incidents.

This book is not about blindly raising fear of technology, but about empowering people to understand how they can master their own destiny in an increasingly computer-driven world, from cybersecurity to new advancements in AI.

In this book, I'll present multiple investigations into how computers can lead to catastrophic outcomes.

I'll additionally guide you through understanding how problems emerge in the technology that shapes much of the modern world around us and the scientific study behind how software engineers work.

As a warning before proceeding, if you're looking for a book which will purely attribute catastrophic failures to technical reasons, you may be sorely disappointed by this book.

The process of researching for this book has taken me inside how catastrophic failures have been covered up (even when it has meant imprisoning innocent people), and how those who speak up have been gagged or faced retaliation.

The reality that becomes apparent throughout this book is that human failures are ultimately those which lead to technical failure. As we get towards the end of the book, we'll begin to explore the remarkable potential humans have to prevent such issues.

One of the key contributions I hope to make through this book is developing your understanding of how killer computers are born and how they can be stopped. Whilst we explore these learnings in the context of computer systems, I believe these apply to other disciplines, including those outside engineering.

The intersection of technology and people is fraught with complexity and potential peril. The stories of Juanita Grossman, Koua Fong Lee and Jean Bookout are not mere anecdotes; they are stark reminders of the tangible impact software can have on human lives.

As a society, we continue to head further into a world where technology is given ever greater levels of trust. Therefore, the importance of understanding this relationship becomes increasingly evident.

Engineers building computer systems play a significant role in helping ensure society is protected from the potential harms of killer computers, but as individuals we also have more power than we think to ensure we don't become victims.

This book aims to peel back the layers of software engineering, going beyond the individual technical factors to the common human factors that ultimately give rise to killer computers. Through this journey, we will explore the multifaceted nature of software – the good, the bad and the potentially dangerous. We will examine case studies, dissect failures and scrutinise the processes that lead to these outcomes.

By understanding what happens behind the scenes, we empower ourselves to make informed decisions so we can protect ourselves from becoming victims to killer computers, advocate for better practices and ultimately shape a future where technology serves humanity, rather than endangers it.

As it would be rude for me not to introduce myself, the next chapter of this book will talk about my own journey and career alongside the challenges that others face as they follow their journey to become software engineers.

From cyberwarfare to planes entering death dives, the subsequent chapters will focus on case studies of catastrophic computer failures and the stories of ethical challenges that underpin them. Throughout this book, I will also discuss what the empirical research says on these matters.

We will conclude with the steps we can take to safeguard ourselves and society at large.

Welcome to a journey into the heart of computer catastrophes and their profound impact on the world, as we strive to ensure that technology ultimately serves humanity, rather than harms it.

# Hello, World!

Scott Adams' "Dilbert" cartoon satirically follows the life of an engineer called Dilbert, showcasing the absurdities of the job. This cartoon strip was later turned into a TV series of the same name.

In one episode, Dilbert recalls his mother taking him to the doctor after he disassembled the TV, clock and stereo, then proceeded to use the parts to produce a "ham radio" (a device that allows the operator to send and receive radio messages with other amateur radio operators).

After the young Dilbert repairs a broken medical diagnostic device in the doctor's office, the doctor diagnoses him with "the knack" for technology: "a rare condition characterised by an extreme intuition about all things electrical and mechanical, and utter social ineptitude".

His mother proceeds to ask the doctor if her son can lead a normal life, but breaks down in tears after the doctor responds, "No, he'll be an engineer."

Recently I saw the medical notes from a child psychiatrist I once saw, and the doctor remarked that my mother "was present at both appointments and her main concerns were Junade's obsession with his computer and spending long hours at night devising software programs".

The doctor described me as "an anxious young man who showed poor eye to eye contact" and "who had very low confidence in himself and his abilities".

All that was missing was the explicit diagnosis of "the knack".

This definition is very different to the type of person I've developed into now. I have long been hesitant to talk about my childhood, however, in September 2023, a journalist for an electronics engineering publication called *EETimes* decided to look closely into my background. The article was entitled "Hello,

World! School Dropout Is Youngest-Ever IET Fellow".

"Hello, World!" refers to the first computer program that almost all software engineers will ever write – a simple program that will output the text "Hello, World!" onto the screen. This was my first program too.

As I grew up, computers started to become cool and when I left school, I became a software engineer.

Ironically, I started my professional life working in the mental health space. I worked on engineering IT internal systems for a professional body of counsellors and psychotherapists, alongside building websites for them to market their services to others.

The teaching component of my apprenticeship was done in London, near Old Street Roundabout. The district is known as Silicon Roundabout and at the time the roundabout was lit with billboards from companies like Google, against the backdrop of rooftop antennas from the international satellite telecoms firm Inmarsat. This was my first indication that this could be something big.

From there I had several other software engineering jobs, working on everything from secure data storage systems for banks through to eventually leading the largest development team of any digital agency in the UK.

Nevertheless, I still lacked formal computer qualifications. At one point, the University of Buckingham (the only private university in the country offering a computer science course at the time) offered me a place on their programme following an interview with them, despite my complete lack of school qualifications. However, I would not have been able to afford to take the time out to study and my employer at the time was unwilling to accommodate this.

By the time I was 17, I managed to get myself enrolled in a part-time master's degree course in computer science in the evenings whilst I was working on high-reliability systems in the transportation industry.

At the time, I would drive 90 minutes to work in the morning, then another 90 minutes to university before driving two hours home at night. At the time I was also writing my first book, so I would then work late into the night on this.

Whilst at university, I met Dr Vladimir Dyo, who ultimately supervised my master's project, solving a real-world unsolved problem. This led to my first academic publication. Vladimir later supervised my PhD also. I owe most of my learning how to do academic computer science to Vladimir's supervision.

Then, while working on my degree, I was headhunted by a cybersecurity firm in San Francisco to work at their London office. They flew me out to California for an interview, which turned out to be a few days packed with intensive conversations. This was my first time in the US.

Arriving at San Francisco airport, I remember the US border officer looking suspiciously at me as I told him I was there for a job interview. He referred me to the secondary screening post where another officer asked me about my unusual story in detail (including questioning me as to how, back home, I was doing a master's degree without even having an undergraduate degree).

In the end, he opened up my empty passport and stamped it with entry clearance, wishing me good luck as he did so.

The experience I had of seeing Silicon Roundabout in London was taken to another level when I saw Silicon Valley. I remember walking around at night after the interviews, looking at all the logos of famous technology companies I crossed, thinking that even if I didn't get the job it was worth it to see this. It truly opened my eyes to the scale technology offered.

I did get the job and I worked there for nearly five years, doing some of the best work of my career. My work was being used billions of times every month by people all around the world without them even knowing it. I spent most of my time there as an engineering manager, dealing with several high-stakes situations.

Whilst there I became a Chartered Engineer – something I'd been looking to achieve since working in the high-reliability engineering world. This is the terminal regulatory status for engineers in the UK and confers the power to work in highly regulated parts of engineering. I didn't realise at the time, but at 23 I was the youngest Chartered Engineer on record.

Following working in cybersecurity and that company becoming listed on the New York Stock Exchange, I set up my own consultancy company where I worked on research and transformation initiatives to make software engineering teams happier, whilst allowing them to work more safely and more efficiently. I did this work with some of the largest engineering companies around the world.

My consultancy projects also included cybersecurity work, and I'll share some of this work in relation to North Korea in the next chapter.

Following my PhD and during a brief stint working in finance, I was elected as the youngest Fellow of the Institution of Engineering and Technology on record and, at 27 years old, being believed to be the youngest ever Fellow of any professional engineering institution. My Fellowship was awarded for "significant technological innovation" and "original research" that garnered international recognition.

Since leaving finance and returning to being self-employed, my consultancy practice has moved to focus on investigating and addressing catastrophic software failures and working to address them.

As a relatively new career, software engineers often follow non-traditional routes to joining the profession. Many have an interest in computers, and for us it feels remarkable that we get to spend our days being paid to do what we enjoy.

As software engineering has become an economically prosperous profession, some get pressured into studying computer science and taking a career in the profession, though I have yet to see this work out for anyone in the long run.

Software engineering can be a brutal field to be in. The stress levels are often high and you may find yourself working with people who struggle finding the social skills to navigate conflict. This becomes an ever more testing challenge as you take on middle-management responsibility.

In some environments, a lack of intellectual diversity and empathy can often lead to monocultures developing and sometimes people feeling excluded.

After I did my PhD, I studied psychology at the University of Cambridge. Doing so provided me with a great insight into the different personality disorders and mental health conditions that many people experience, some of which are prevalent in the workplace.

Being a manager within software engineering will often result in having to deal with the undiagnosed mental health issues of people on your team — almost certainly without any qualifications to do so and without the support of your own management.

On one of my engineering teams, I once had a severely autistic engineer with issues building up that successive managers had failed to address. When I asked her previous manager about it, he retorted, "That's often just an excuse for people to be a dick."

She would constantly use alien emojis in her messages, but it wasn't until long after I'd left the team that I realised she used them because they represented how she felt — like an alien.

Another engineer who I once recruited told me after I hired her that she didn't need the glasses she wore during the interview, but that they helped with her own mental health challenges.

Similarly, many people have their own unresolved trauma and personal issues and seek to transfer that to others in the way they may have felt when they were younger.

I've heard of colleagues leaving their jobs or the profession altogether after being screamed at by managers or bullied by co-workers, alongside experiencing blatant discrimination.

I have witnessed several similar instances in my own career. Early in my career, a senior member of staff once threatened to reach over the table and smack me across the face. On another occasion, I was subject to a lengthy screaming session by a manager.

That said, there are many great people in the profession who have enormous depths of empathy in their hearts and who have taught me a great deal.

Additionally, the profession provides an opportunity which few find elsewhere: the ability to change the world in a substantial way.

I've been proud not only of my own achievements but also to see the careers of others I've helped to develop who have gone on to achieve massive things in their own right. It is a hugely rewarding experience to provide others with your engineering worldview and allow them to cherry-pick what they take forward to become their own.

# Cyberwar

It was the start of August 2021, and I was transiting through Charles de Gaulle Airport in France. I'd left my home in Scotland but my long journey had just begun.

As I was walking through the transit security, one of the security officers said to me, "*Français? Anglais?*" ("French? English?")

Whilst placing my baggage on a tray, I replied, "*Parlez-vous anglais?*" ("Do you speak English?")

The rest of the interaction proceeded with me responding in French to his questions in English. It felt oddly satisfying though. With the pandemic having halted travel, it had been a long while since I'd used any other language except English and the programming languages used to write code for computers.

I boarded my next flight, which was an almost empty Boeing 777 to Seoul, South Korea. After a few hours, I was eating a

French breakfast whilst we flew down the coast of the Korean peninsula from China.

I felt uncomfortable looking at the inflight map and seeing the names of North Korean towns appear.

Uncomfortable not only because many of the residents below would never get to leave their own province (let alone ever fly on an airplane), but also because some of the names of towns I recognised because they shared names with concentration camps which operated there.

When I got off, I switched my broken French for my even worse Korean. I was here for six weeks but I would spend a significant amount of the start of the trip in a government quarantine facility, despite having had my COVID-19 vaccinations in the UK.

My willingness to spend time in a quarantine facility to visit South Korea had resulted from what I was seeing online. I had spent the last few months helping journalists from NK News track what was going on online in

North Korea. Stories I'd initially helped with included the activities of North Korea's state sponsored hackers, how North Koreans were doing at online coding competitions and how a botched server upgrade took some of North Korea's few public-facing websites offline.

Once out of quarantine, I began to travel up to the border between South Korea and North Korea. One of the starkest reminders of the tension on the Korean peninsula is seeing the perimeter of the country lined with barbed wire, especially coming from an island nation where no such fences exist.

Another reminder is seeing conscripts dressed in army uniform in public, again not a common occurrence in Britain where the military is rarely seen in uniform in public.

I travelled by bus from Seoul to Gyeonggi Province in the north of South Korea. From there, I somehow managed to navigate my way onto the deserted shuttle bus up to Odusan Unification Tower – one of the few open observatories in the country, giving an insight into North Korea.

Many associate the border between South Korea and North Korea with the Joint Security Area, where photos show tense-looking soldiers from both sides facing each other down beside military huts. However, much of the border is actually eerily peaceful.

The Odusan Unification Tower is set in tranquil surroundings by the shore, on a river separating the two Koreas. The only hint of this being the border of two countries technically at war is the barbed wire on the shoreline.

I can't remember how long I spent there, looking into North Korea through the telescope.

But then I noticed something significant. Across the border, a soldier was cycling to an unattended guard post. From what I had heard, in the past these kinds of border movements have been associated with missile launches. There were rumours of tensions increasing and from what I saw, the internet infrastructure in North Korea was looking increasingly unstable.

Indeed, military movements were afoot, and towards the end of August, outages of North Korea's internet infrastructure started to align with test missile launches.

Over the coming months, I began to see key news websites with sources inside North Korea targeted by increasingly sophisticated hacks. For example, *Daily NK*, which the BBC used to communicate with sources in North Korea for a 2023 documentary, was hacked.

Work I did with NK News helped to improve the security of the website in the aftermath by raising attention to other potential security vulnerabilities.

Other sophisticated attacks were launched against journalists and others observing North Korea.

A few months later, towards the start of 2022, I was back in my flat in Scotland when, late one night, I noticed what appeared to be large-scale cyber-attacks hitting North Korea, eerily coinciding with when the country was launching missile tests.

Many North Korea watchers became concerned as to whether the international community had the bandwidth to deal with two potential international crises, the developing situation in Ukraine (Vladimir Putin would invade Ukraine less than a month later) alongside the new tensions developing in North Korea.

These attacks took North Korea's internet infrastructure completely offline, meaning that web traffic in and out of the country was put to a halt.

By the 26th of January, I saw a second attack in just two weeks. It was so powerful it made it impossible to route data into North Korea.

The attack used is known as a Distributed Denial of Service (DDoS) attack. These attacks work by overwhelming a computer or network with so much junk traffic that they are unable to handle it and so legitimate traffic is blocked.

The attack facing North Korea was so powerful that it was taking offline the key internet routers that would allow traffic in and out of the country, taking North Korea off the global routing table of the internet.

NK News published this story and quickly after the Reuters news agency also picked it up, with it then going on to make international headlines around the world.

Journalists began asking South Korean government officials about the attack, and they simply responded with, "We are monitoring the situation under coordination with relevant government agencies."

Speculation was mounting as to who was behind these attacks. Some speculated that it was a western intelligence agency behind the attacks. At times, the attacks would happen before the missile launches were publicly known about, suggesting inside knowledge or that the missile launches were in retaliation to the cyberattacks.

This story attracted international attention, and whilst I told journalists that the North Korean internet outages seemed to be caused by attacks, I refused to answer their requests for me to attribute a particular actor to the group, as I just didn't know the answer.

Later, Andy Greenberg, a journalist from *WIRED* magazine contacted me to say he knew who the hacker was and had been in contact after following the story, with the attacker having shared evidence of their responsibility with him.

*WIRED* later reported that a lone American hacker, going by the pseudonym P4x, had taken responsibility for these attacks as revenge for being targeted by their hackers. The article was entitled "North Korea Hacked Him. So He Took Down Its Internet".

The attacker claimed to be doing this as revenge. North Korean state hackers will often run campaigns to gather money, intelligence or simply to cause havoc. North Korea had been targeting hackers to attempt to steal their secret hacking techniques (known as zero-days) for their own campaigns.

After the information about this hacking campaign became public, P4x realised he was a victim of these attacks. After realising no one would be willing to help him get justice and after a year of allowing his anger to brew, he started launching these attacks against North Korea.

Andy Greenberg wrote: "… responsibility for North Korea's ongoing internet outages doesn't lie with US Cyber Command or any other state-sponsored hacking agency. In fact, it was the work of one American man in a T-shirt, pyjama pants, and slippers, sitting in his living room night after night, watching Alien movies and eating spicy corn snacks—and periodically walking over to his home office to check on the progress of the programs he was running to disrupt the internet of an entire country."

Following the publication of this story, the missile launches stopped and the missile situation in North Korea calmed.

A significant proportion of my career has been spent working in cybersecurity, building safeguards to stop hackers from stealing data, taking critical systems offline and defacing websites. During many of the most high-profile global geopolitical events in the past few years, I've had a significant role to play in ensuring cybersecurity – but this is one of the few situations I am able to talk publicly about.

People are often curious to ask me what the internet in North Korea is used for. Whilst access to the broader global internet is highly restricted in North Korea, I have been able to track some of the internet traffic coming and going from the country and it's interesting to see what kind of content North Koreans who are privileged to have this access will download. This includes TV series like *Squid Game* and movies from the *Harry Potter* franchise.

The reason North Korea originally targeted P4x was he was amongst a set of security researchers who North Korea wanted to steal their research from to use in their own attacks.

The particular research they were after was what are known as "zero-day" vulnerabilities. These security vulnerabilities are techniques that are not known to anyone else so have not been patched by security updates.

Security vulnerabilities in general leverage mistakes in how software has been written in order to get it to do something it shouldn't. For example, an attacker could use a vulnerability to gain access to a system that they should not have, or to gain greater levels of access.

Sophisticated zero-day attacks could simply involve a text message being sent to someone's phone, which in turn results in their device being fully compromised, without any interaction from the user.

More often than not, however, some level of interaction is needed from the user in order to compromise a device. This leverages a technique called "phishing" to get a user to click a link, install software, forgo a password or otherwise behave in a way they shouldn't.

This is done by a technique known as "social engineering", where someone is convinced to do something they shouldn't, maybe by an email or text message that isn't really from who the email says it's from.

When these attacks are targeted within companies, a single employee being compromised can then lead to a chain reaction where key pieces of secret information are compromised. Many organisations will have internal security teams to detect and contain these attacks, but some will either fall through the cracks or not have such teams.

Once within a company's internal network, the attackers can get to work gaining more access and exfiltrating data.

This was the fate of a website known as Ashley Madison – a dating site dedicated to facilitating extramarital affairs.

In July 2015, Ashley Madison fell victim to a massive cyberattack. A group called "The Impact Team" infiltrated the site's security systems and accessed sensitive data belonging to millions of users. The hackers demanded that the site be taken down, threatening to release the personal information of users if their demands were not met.

When Ashley Madison and its parent company Avid Life Media (ALM) did not comply with the ultimatum, the hackers made good on their threat. They published a trove of data, including usernames, email addresses, credit card details and even intimate personal details that had been shared on the platform.

Alongside the data, the hackers posted a message under the heading "Time's up!" stating: "We have explained the fraud, deceit, and stupidity of ALM and their members. Now everyone gets to see their data."

The consequences of the hack were far-reaching and devastating. Individuals who had used the site faced public humiliation and personal crises as their private affairs were exposed. Relationships and families were torn apart, careers were jeopardised and the breach of privacy had a profound psychological impact on many.

Tragically, the fallout from the hack included reports of suicides linked to the exposure of personal information. Law enforcement and media outlets reported that at least two individuals associated with the leaked data took their own lives. The incident served as a stark reminder of the real–world consequences of cyberattacks and the importance of digital security and privacy.

In addition to the personal tragedies, the hack prompted a slew of lawsuits against Avid Life Media. Users sought compensation for the emotional distress and reputational damage caused by the breach. The company faced scrutiny over its security practices and the authenticity of its privacy guarantees, which had assured users that their information was secure and confidential.

The Ashley Madison hack stands as one of the most notorious cybercrimes in history, not only for the scale of the breach but also for the deeply personal nature of the data exposed and the subsequent impact on the lives of the individuals involved.

In 2023, a documentary called *The Ashley Madison Affair* streamed on Disney+ in which a number of friends of mine who are cybersecurity experts were interviewed about the data breach.

In the documentary, a new theory was presented that a disgruntled former employee could have been behind the attack, but this and other theories have not yet been proven true. To date, the culprit behind the hack remains a mystery.

Even if the culprit is identified, depending on the legal jurisdiction in question, too much time may well have passed for criminal charges to be brought, making the prospect of justice even more remote.

When a website is compromised through a data breach, that can have a domino effect onto a high-risk, higher-security website.

For example, if the website you order pizza from was either compromised or someone was able to obtain your password to it in a different way, but you also used the same password for online banking, the compromise of a low-risk website can lead to a significant security breach.

If passwords aren't stored securely, then they can be stolen to compromise other websites which use the same password.

Typically, when a website stores a password, it should be stored in a way the original password is no longer known but it can be checked if the password is correct when the user provides it. This is known as hashing. Unfortunately, in many cases this is either poorly implemented or not implemented at all.

Additionally, weaker passwords can often be cracked through guessing attacks by either trying them on a website that doesn't limit the number of attempts, or using an unlimited number of attacks once a data breach has occurred.

Additionally, until recently, cybersecurity advice was to use highly complex but very hard to remember passwords. This led to users being incentivised to use the same password for all sites, so they didn't have to remember multiple complex ones.

I worked on this problem a number of years ago by inventing a way that someone could check if their password is in a data breach without ever needing to share the password with a third-party, or even the full hash of the password.

Since then, this technology has been implemented into password managers like 1Password, web browsers like Google Chrome and Apple devices, amongst a vast variety of other online services and tools.

Research I led found that when users were presented with warnings telling them their passwords were in a data breach and were given good advice, they were significantly more likely to take corrective actions.

So how can you protect yourself from these kinds of attacks? First, use a password manager. A password manager allows you to store a unique randomly generated password for each site, with your password vault controlled by a single master password. Set your master password to something secure but memorable, for example by choosing three completely random words.

This means if one website is compromised, the attackers won't have access to the others. At the same time, you'll have the benefit of only needing to remember one password.

Second, it is increasingly common to use two-factor authentication, whereby you generate a code from a different device when you need to login to a website. This is a good security practice, and you should enable it.

However, if you get these codes via text message, there are a variety of targeted attacks where hackers try to take control of your phone number in order to receive the code.

This can be done by tricking your phone provider into giving your phone number to someone else, intercepting your phone signal or by physically taking the SIM card out of your phone.

This last example was the fate that faced Charlotte Morgan, who experienced a thief stealing from her while she was at the gym. The thief managed to break into her locker and, despite different PINs and passwords for her bank accounts and phone, they gained access to her money.

You might think that your phone's fingerprint or facial recognition, or even your PIN, would stop thieves from getting to your text messages. However, these security features have a critical flaw; they don't always protect against someone simply taking the SIM card out of your phone and using it in another device.

Whilst it's often possible to use an app instead of text messages for getting these codes, many companies and services do not support this because these apps can have a worse user experience (particularly if someone loses their phone). Therefore, they focus on targeting the security benefits to the maximum number of users and will solely use text messages to deliver these codes.

However, if you're comfortable, using a dedicated authenticator app (or even a dedicated authenticator device like something called a Yubikey) is the more secure option. These devices use maths to generate the code, meaning there's no communication to be intercepted.

However, in many cases text message is the only option for receiving login codes. This is where setting a SIM card PIN becomes important. It is an extra code that locks your SIM card, so if someone tries to use it in another phone, they'll need the PIN to unlock it. Without it, they can't use your SIM to receive your texts or calls.

For iPhone users, you can set this up in your settings under "Mobile Data", and for Android users, it's under "Security". This simple step adds another layer of security.

This risk is partially mitigated through the use of eSIMs, where devices like the latest iPhones in the United States don't have a SIM card slot but instead use software to store this phone network information. Nevertheless, setting up a SIM PIN is still possible on eSIMs and a good idea for added security against more sophisticated attacks.

While we often have to rely on less secure methods like text message for one-time passwords, it's important we do what we can to protect ourselves, and a SIM PIN is a straightforward yet effective measure.

Turning to other security measures, you should be particularly careful about protecting your email account. This is often one of the most valuable things for an attacker to own as they can, in many cases, then reset passwords without needing to know any other passwords. Email is also often how you are told when someone is trying to gain access to your account.

Earlier we discussed phishing attacks; the typical advice is to keep an eye out for suspicious emails, which often try to create a false sense of urgency and may well not use specific information or poor spelling and grammar.

However, over the years I've been in cybersecurity, there are some highly sophisticated phishing attacks I've encountered, known as spear-phishing.

The attackers can offer highly personal information and present themselves well. In other cases, due to the sheer number of attempts scammers will make, they can target you better.

Imagine you go online to renew your life insurance, and then within minutes you receive a call about your life insurance. You are then potentially far more likely to be convinced by a scam. The volume of attacks the scammers make means they will eventually stumble upon someone in the right place and the right time.

Data science approaches can then be used to make these attacks more targeted by identifying the times when people are most likely to fall for such scams. For example, a payroll scam in the UK could be targeted at the end of the month when most employees get paid. This is why it's important to be cautious, even if something seems like it's the right time.

Be careful to avoid taking people at face value if they provide no evidence to prove who they say they are. Even if they are able to provide evidence, be cautious, nevertheless.

If something like this happens on the phone, feel free to hang up and call back using an official number. For example, if dealing with your bank, use the number on the back of your bank card.

Governments often maintain ways people can report suspicious phone calls, text messages and emails to keep others safe. It's worth looking up what your local government suggests as the way of doing this.

For example, in the US, phishing emails can be forwarded to *reportphishing@apwg.org*. In the UK, they can be forwarded to *report@phishing.gov.uk*. In the UK and US, you can also forward scam text messages to 7726. In the UK, scam phone calls can also be sent to this number by texting the word 'Call' followed by the phone number to 7726. In the US, fraud calls can be reported online at *ReportFraud.ftc.gov*.

Protecting yourself from more sophisticated attacks can be tough, but there are steps you can take here, too.

Commonly, hackers will distribute computer viruses which will encrypt the contents of your computer and then demand a ransom to get your files back. In many cases the files will not be recovered even after the ransom has been paid.

This highlights the critical importance of ensuring key files are backed up to an online cloud service or an external hard drive. This also helps if something goes wrong with your computer, or files are lost by mistake.

Finally, when it comes to protecting yourself from highly sophisticated attackers, the single best step you can take is keeping your computer and any apps up to date, as these updates contain essential security updates when zero-day vulnerabilities become public.

Of course, be careful about installing suspicious software on your computer in general and avoid websites which trick you into installing software by pretending to be a security update.

If you're buying a second-hand device, make sure the manufacturer still supports it with security updates by checking online.

Finally, always be cautious about the information you share with third-party websites in case the information is compromised, like in the Ashley Madison case. Reputable companies will have strong security teams, but data breaches do happen to the largest organisations, so attempt to minimise risk by controlling which information you share.

Additionally, reputable companies will usually be transparent when a security compromise is detected and those who are less reputable may seek to cover up security flaws. So, within limits, transparency on security issues from a company is no indication they are less secure than others.

Following these simple pieces of advice will help keep your data secure and protect you from the vast majority of security attacks you're likely to ever face.

In the most extreme situations – for example, if you ever find yourself potentially being targeted by a highly sophisticated threat actor, like a government or non-state intelligence agency – there are steps you can take here too. However, it is worth either researching security measures in more detail or gaining specialist advice.

In these situations, it is essential to compartmentalise risk. Security researchers will often have a dedicated device they use for work or high-risk activities, which is separate from their personal computer. Some will use virtual computers or sandboxes in order to compartmentalise risks, but these have their limits and can sometimes be worked around, so a separate device is the safer option.

Additionally, Apple devices now feature a "Lockdown Mode" which can enable high levels of security for people under such threat. Similarly, Google offers an "Advanced Protection Program" for such instances.

Hopefully you'll never find yourself in such a situation where you need this level of protection.

One of the things I always find remarkable about cybersecurity is how it fascinates people beyond when there is an accidental failure explanation for something.

Often when a technical failure occurs, the media is quick to try and find a malicious angle like a hack to attribute it to. Murder stories tend to grip people more than accidents.

I have many memories of being an on-call engineer when a piece of critical national infrastructure goes online. Surprisingly quickly the media as well as people on social media platforms look to connect the issue to some form of an attack, even when the root cause was more benign.

Upon returning home from Korea, I saw subsequent outages from North Korea's internet which I attributed to botched server upgrades instead of anything malicious. Of course, such stories only got minimal press attention compared to those I'd attributed to attacks – not least as these were of far less geopolitical significance.

Evolutionary psychologists will attribute this to a human need to learn what makes criminals tick in order to protect ourselves in the future.

However, even when things seem like an innocent technical mistake, frequently there is something more sinister beneath the surface. We'll explore the level of cover-up needed for such negligence to persist later in this book.

In the next chapter, I want to turn to why software has been leading growth in the world, and how the public's expectations are changing. This will lay the foundations for us to understand the context of killer computers, both past and present.

# Sustainability

I set up my most recent business in September 2023 after seeing a significant trend emerging in the software industry.

In the past, delivering ever-faster innovation and staying ahead of the market has been the priority.

Following the 2009 financial crisis, bank interest rates reached record lows, allowing companies to raise or borrow money cheaply, and investors turned to putting money in tech where the returns outweighed what they could get from saving. Since then, computer software has seen ever more explosive growth as more of the world moves to leveraging technology to remove friction.

In 2011, Marc Andreessen, the co-founder and general partner of the venture capital firm Andreessen Horowitz, put it simply: "Software is eating the world."

Evidence for this claim can be seen in how technology like social media platforms such as Facebook and TikTok, streaming services including Netflix and e-commerce platforms like Amazon have changed the world.

The first iPhone was launched in January 2007, but the true power of software showed in the App Store, launched by Apple in July 2008. This fundamentally transformed the iPhone from a technology-rich mobile device into a versatile platform in its own right.

Prior to the App Store, the iPhone's capabilities were largely confined to the applications Apple provided. Users were unable to install third-party software, which limited the phone's functionality and customisation.

Suddenly, software engineers had a direct channel to millions of users, and the barriers to entry for creating mobile applications were drastically lowered. This democratisation of app development led to an explosion of creativity and innovation. The variety of apps available ranged from the practical, such as navigation and banking apps, to the entertaining, like games and social networking. This diversity turned the iPhone into a digital Swiss Army knife, capable of adapting to the unique needs and preferences of its users.

The role of high-speed mobile internet has helped extend this technology into every crevice of our lives.

Not only can we use our mobile phones to get transport instructions, but also access live bus times and traffic data from sensors embedded into the physical world without us noticing. We can also track our taxi drivers and food deliveries in real time on our mobile devices.

We can preheat our cars in the mornings from our mobile phones and even connect our washing machines to the internet.

Sending money no longer requires a chequebook or a visit to the bank, as mobile banking brings convenience to your phone. You can even make contactless payments from your mobile without needing to handle your credit card.

In England, citizens can use the app of the National Health Service (NHS) to access their medical records, book appointments and even register their organ donation decisions.

However, like an iceberg, there is more of this technology that powers our lives that can first be seen, from power plants to water treatment facilities. Software and Artificial Intelligence are becoming even more deeply embedded into every aspect of our lives.

The COVID-19 pandemic saw yet more huge swaths of life move online. Working from home brought more people to use video conferencing, whilst contact tracing apps and vaccination record systems pushed more of our data online. At the same time, tech companies binged on hiring as many engineers as they could during the first half of the COVID-19 pandemic.

In January 2022, there was only one major UK high-street store that did not use e-commerce: the clothing chain Primark. On their website, a frequently asked question of "Do you have an online shop?" was met with the reply: "Unfortunately we currently do not offer an online shop. Primark products are available in our stores only. Click here to find out where your nearest store is!"

However, that article is now long gone, and you can now order Primark clothes online too.

The need to rapidly deliver innovation was so great that Marc Andreessen commented in 2014 that: "Cycle time compression may be the most underestimated force in determining winners and losers in tech."

Cycle time refers to how long it takes from starting work on a new feature to getting it in front of users. Some engineering teams can do this in a matter of minutes thanks to the power of software.

However, the wind is changing.

Following the end of the pandemic, inflation was up and central banks raised interest rates in an attempt to combat this. The cost of borrowing money became higher, investors needed higher returns to beat inflation, company expenses increased and consumers had less money to spend.

This meant the previously bottomless pit of money for tech companies now had a limit. Instead of loss-making high-growth companies being the rage, profitable businesses became desirable.

Against this backdrop, in 2023 I began to notice that consumers, having seen society go through massive shifts during the pandemic, were less tolerant of change.

One of the first insights I had into this was in January 2023 when I was in Japan to speak at a conference.

When I visited Japan a few years prior, its society was rule oriented and highly averse to uncertainty. Many engineers held Japan up as a gold standard of agility in the engineering process.

However, I quickly noticed that this had changed. Having never been on a late train in Japan, the first train I boarded from the airport to my Tokyo city centre hotel was delayed. And even in this rule-oriented society, after the end of the pandemic people weren't following the government's guidance to wear masks less frequently due to the risk of heatstroke.

Before returning home I had to go to a ticket office to change a train ticket. Standing in line, I noticed the employee behind the desk would bow to every customer she would serve but none would bow back. Unthinkable a few years ago.

One reason I found this interesting was that in September 2022, when Queen Elizabeth II was lying in state in the UK – with guards standing at each corner with heads bowed and weapons inverted, facing away from the casket – the British public also seemed to depart from their own bowing culture but in a very different direction.

In the UK, even in the presence of a king or queen, etiquette dictates that you never bow more than your head (a neck bow) or do more than a small curtsy. However, watching people pay their tributes to the Queen, many departed from this tradition, feeling an urge to bow their entire bodies.

I was being shown a part of rural northern Japan by a Japanese guide who had once worked in disaster relief for the US embassy in the country. I asked her about whether she felt Japanese culture was changing, and she agreed the culture had changed and felt it was the pandemic that had led to this.

After, she turned to me and said, "But you know, this is true in Europe too." Having recently come back from a holiday in Italy, she told me how remarkable she found it that the country had quickly adopted contactless payments and other changes within the culture.

Perhaps I am myself part of this movement, having left my flat in the bustle of London for a quieter home in Scotland during the pandemic.

Research provides some interesting insight into how these cultural factors apply to computer systems.

Between the 29th of September 2023 and the 8th of October 2023, I conducted a representative opinion poll of the British public with the help of the market research firm Survation. Survation is a member of the British Polling Council and abides by its rules.

We asked a representative sample of 1,989 UK adults questions about their attitudes to computer software. This provided us 95% confidence that the "true" result would fall within 2.2% of what the study told us.

When we looked at what factors mattered to the public "to a great extent" when using computer systems, data security came top with 62%. The second most important factors were avoiding serious bugs and the importance of data accuracy (both at 55%).

Just 28% said having software that was highly customised to their needs mattered to them "to a great extent", with 28% also saying the same of getting the latest technology. Surprisingly, only 22% said getting the latest features as quickly as possible mattered "to a great extent".

One of the reasons these results were so remarkable was that they flew in the face of what the traditional metrics frameworks said mattered when measuring software delivery performance.

With Survation, I also interviewed 280 software engineers in the UK about their attitudes towards reliability.

Software engineers themselves also placed delivering work quickly as the thing which mattered least when considering what mattered most about their jobs among eight different job factors, with just 33% saying this mattered "to a great extent".

Software reliability (51%) and keeping data secure (47%) were the most important factors, except for being able to provide for themselves and their families (52%).

Concern amongst software engineers regarding reliability has been growing. I compared my results from the 2023 survey with my June 2021 Survation poll of 258 UK software engineers.

In 2021, 57% agreed that software reliability at their workplace concerned them to a "great" or "moderate" extent. Over two years later, my 2023 polling found that 71% agreed – meaning there had been a 25% increase.

Looking at the percentage who were concerned about software reliability at their workplace only "to a great extent", 34% agreed in 2023, up from 20% in 2021. A 68% increase in the number of software engineers concerned about software reliability at their workplace "to a great extent" over just two years.

Before this research was published, when I returned to consultancy work in 2023, almost all my clients were attempting to capitalise on this trend for software reliability, as their market research (and that of their investors) was clearly showing positive signals there. This included companies attempting to use Artificial Intelligence to detect security and safety issues in code, to those trying to get automated software reliability tests to run more efficiently, to those trying to prevent software projects being delayed.

The scientific work and the conversions I had demonstrated to me that times were changing. Software reliability was becoming increasingly important.

In the start of 2024, the public outcry about the Post Office Horizon IT scandal discussed in the next chapter truly underlines the scale of this.

# Falsely Imprisoned

I began to look closely at the Post Office Horizon IT scandal in the first half of 2022.

At the time I was writing a weekly column in *ComputerWeekly* and when I met the editor for the first time, as we ate our fish lunch in a restaurant with a panoramic view overlooking the City of London, he told me with pride about the success they had achieved in campaigning for justice on this story. Of course, there was still far more left to do.

*ComputerWeekly* has campaigned on this story since 2009. As of February 2024, I count the number of articles they have written on this topic at 367.

This story is certainly worthy of this level of coverage. It has been referred to as "the most widespread miscarriage of justice in UK history", with those wrongly imprisoned including a pregnant woman. Multiple suicides have also been attributed to this.

The Horizon IT scandal is a stark illustration of the catastrophic consequences that occur when technology fails, institutions refuse to accept responsibility and cover-ups ensue.

The British Post Office is how many UK citizens do their business with the state. Before April 2024, if you needed an International Driving Permit, only the Post Office could issue them. People collect benefits and pensions from the Post Office, and with high-street banks closing and the growth in online-only banks, many offer their services through the Post Office. The Post Office can even check your passport application and send it off to His Majesty's Passport Office for you.

The Post Office is incorporated as a private company, but there is only one shareholder: the British government.

Some branches are operated directly by the company Post Office Limited (known as "Crown offices"), however others are franchised out to subpostmasters (often referred to as "postmasters" for simplicity).

Postmasters play an essential role in their communities and are often viewed as people of good character who are highly trusted by their community to provide access to critical services.

In running a Post Office, postmasters will even sign the Official Secrets Act – the law which swears MI6 spies to lifetime secrecy.

Described as the largest non-military IT contract in Europe, the Horizon IT system was, in essence, the digital backbone of the Post Office's day-to-day transactions. With the rollout starting in 1999, the accounting software was designed to meticulously track the flow of money in and out of each Post Office branch. From stamp sales to utility bill payments, Horizon was supposed to ensure that every penny was accounted for.

In 2009, the Post Office told *ComputerWeekly* that: "Horizon is an extremely robust system which operates over our entire Post Office network and successfully records millions of transactions each day. There is no evidence that points to any fault with the technology. We would always look into and investigate any issues raised by subpostmasters."

The Horizon IT system, developed by Fujitsu, was introduced with the promise of revolutionising the Post Office's operations. Yet, almost from the outset, it was plagued with glitches and errors that had dire consequences for many postmasters.

The system began to erroneously show shortfalls, sometimes amounting to thousands of pounds, in the accounts of various Post Office branches. These discrepancies could not be explained by the postmasters, many of whom had been running their branches successfully for years, if not decades.

In the days before broadband internet was mainstream, the Horizon IT system was a highly complex distributed system. It sought to be able to consolidate data in a centralised database between sometimes numerous terminals in a Post Office.

For computer scientists, even when software is written perfectly, systems which are distributed across multiple computers are a tough problem. It is notably hard to be able to achieve data consistency, system availability and separation of data all in one go, even in a theoretical distributed system (this is known by computer scientists as the CAP theorem).

However, Horizon was a flawed system in its own right. Another government agency, the Benefits Agency, pulled out from the project during its development, fundamentally changing the project's requirements.

There was limited documentation of system requirements, and the software was essentially built on the foundation of a prototype using a software development approach designed to prioritise speed.

David McDonnell, a former engineering manager at Fujitsu, was in charge of running the team responsible for the EPOS (electronic point of sale) system for a brief period of time during 1998.

In his evidence presented during the ongoing public inquiry into the scandal, he wrote of his experience of taking on the team that:

> *Within days of starting it became very obvious that:*
>
>     a. *[The existing manager] had immense knowledge of how the post office worked but was not technical and had no formal*

*qualifications in software development.*

b.  *There were no development standards or methodology, coding practices, peer reviews, unit testing standards or design specifications in place. In fact, this team was like the Wild West.*

c.  *Several of the development team were not capable of producing professional code.*

When asked by the inquiry what McDonnell meant by his statement that the team was "like the Wild West", he replied:

*Pretty much as it says on the tin. There were no standards in place, there were no design documents. The culture of the development team was— I wouldn't say it was a holiday camp, but it was free format. There was no structure, no discipline; it was crazy, never seen anything like it.*

The inquiry also asked McDonnell, "You say that several of the development team were not capable of producing professional code. Did that impact your view on the integrity of the EPOS system?"

McDonnell replied:

> *Fundamentally. If they weren't capable of demonstrating to me or an auditor or anybody else in the building that they could write a simple piece of code in a professional standard, then I had to ask myself: what have they been writing for the last 12 months or however long they've been there? What's under the bonnet in the system already that they've contributed?*

When asked about the approach to fixing bugs, McDonnell said:

> *So what was happening was the project, or the EPOSS counter team, had got into such an exhausted state that the culture had become: throw a fix in the code,*

*throw it over the fence at the test team. There was very little control of the release mechanism from the development team into the test team.*

In February 2021, *ComputerWeekly* reported that a senior software developer who worked on building the Horizon system for Fujitsu raised similar accusations, but additionally claimed "that senior managers at Fujitsu were aware that an important element of the Horizon system did not function correctly and could not be fixed".

Back in the Post Offices, when the postmasters faced a shortfall they had no option on the computer but to make good the loss themselves or carry it forward to the next accounting period. If the shortfall wasn't made good, the Post Office couldn't open the next day.

It wasn't until long after the scandal became public that the journalist Nick Wallis reported that the ability to challenge a discrepancy was added.

The Post Office held the postmasters responsible for any losses, on the basis of their franchise contract. A judge later noted that the Post Office took the approach of inverting the burden of proof such that the accused had to prove that no loss had occurred.

The Horizon support desk wasn't much help, either. An insider, Amandeep Singh, told the public inquiry of the toxic environment in the call centre where employees were mocked. He reported that when South Asian postmasters would call to ask for help, shouts could be heard of: "I have another Patel scamming again!"

Singh went on to say, "They mocked Scottish and Welsh postmasters and pretended they could not understand them. They created a picture of postmasters that suggested they were incompetent or fraudsters."

There were reported instances of the shortfalls doubling after attempts were made to correct discrepancies.

Postmaster Chhaya Patel told the inquiry:

> *I remember one shortfall that was in the region of £1,600.00 that was apparently a shortfall in my cash [drawer]. I received a transaction correction which I settled on the Horizon system as I could not afford for the system to be down. I called the helpline and followed their instructions but this resulted in the shortfall doubling to about £3,200.00.*

Post Office would direct auditors to visit branches following discrepancies in the Horizon system, then send out demand letters for the money to be repaid.

Many postmasters therefore resorted to borrowing money from their own business in order to fill the imaginary shortfalls the computer was making. Some went into debt, remortgaging their houses and even being made bankrupt.

To the public inquiry, Mary Philip of Fife, Scotland spoke of how, within weeks after her mother took over the Post Office, there would be repeated shortfalls ranging from a few pounds to a few thousand pounds. When she reported this, the Post Office told her she was the only one experiencing such issues.

Ironically, in 2021 Mary found out that the lawyer her mother hired to help "had another client with the same problems but could not divulge that at the time due to client confidentiality".

During the weekly tally of accounts, when shortfalls were re-calculated, "the missing amounts were never the same twice".

Mary wrote in her witness statement:

> *The final consequence came early one Thursday morning. ... [Post Office] auditors arrived at the branch around*

7.30 a.m. They demanded to be let into the branch. They immediately went to the cash drawer.

The night before there had been a £94 shortfall and rather than stay up half the night and re-run the tally, my mother, honest as ever, wrote a £94 personal cheque and put it in the drawer, thinking she was making sure the branch was not suffering a cash shortfall.

That, however, was her downfall. She was immediately told she was suspended, because it was taken to be proof that she was mis-accounting and fraudulently making good money she had withdrawn from the PO.

I recall her walking out of the branch and crossing the road to her car and being chased across the road by an auditor (I cannot recall his name). She was told aggressively the only reason

However, the situation gets worse.

The Post Office Investigation Branch is the oldest recognised criminal investigation force in the world. However, as the Post Office themselves admit, they have no special power to bring criminal prosecutions.

Rather uniquely in the world, the legal system in England, Wales and Northern Ireland allows private individuals and companies to bring their own criminal prosecutions. A company can be the victim, the investigator and the prosecutor. The Post Office leveraged this ability in England and Wales.

Whilst the power of private citizens to prosecute also technically exists in Scotland, it requires special circumstances to be evident in the crime and for permission to be granted from the highest criminal court in Scotland, the High Court of Justiciary. In the 20th century, such permission was only granted twice.

Nevertheless, the Scottish prosecutor lists some "specialist reporting agencies" who act as investigators and refer crimes to the prosecutor themselves, rather than through the police. The Post Office is one such agency and has leveraged this route to achieve prosecutions.

In Northern Ireland, the police force and prosecution authority conducted prosecutions following investigations carried out by the Post Office.

When shortfalls emerged in the Horizon IT system, the Post Office blamed the postmasters. They would commence investigations and prosecutions for accusations such as theft, fraud and false accounting.

The Lord Advocate, the most senior legal advisor in Scotland, said in a January 2024 statement:

> *During this period, the Post Office did not disclose to Scottish prosecutors the true extent of the Horizon problems as they are now known to be. Scottish prosecutors received assurances that the system was robust. These were assurances that prosecutors, without the benefit of hindsight, were entitled to take at face value. They would not have known, nor indeed suspected, that the Post Office may not have been revealing the true extent of the Horizon problems.*

Nevertheless, the Scottish prosecution service claims they took action when they became aware of the issues to prevent miscarriages of justice. Accordingly, the number affected may well be less than in England and Wales.

In one 2014 case, a Scottish prosecutor in Glasgow refused to prosecute two sisters

(Jacquie El Kasaby and Rose Stewart) over Horizon IT issues. Nevertheless, after the case was thrown out the Post Office continued to pursue the shortfall as a debt without telling the sisters of the reason for the failed prosecution.

Later that year the BBC reports there was another prosecution in Scotland using Horizon data. However, in 2015 Scottish prosecutors stopped the prosecution of such cases (although previously prosecuted cases weren't reviewed until the scale of the problem was truly known following an English court case over the accuracy of Horizon in 2015).

In England and Wales, postmasters would often find themselves accused of theft and false accounting, despite there being no evidence of theft. On the basis that the accused would plead guilty to false accounting and would not blame the Horizon IT system, the charges of theft would be dropped. Essentially using an unsubstantiated criminal charge for plea bargaining purposes.

Post Office investigators would descend on a branch, taking the postmaster to a centrally-run Crown office Post Office to use as a makeshift interrogation suite. Before the Post Office split from Royal Mail, Royal Mail offices were also used. In some cases, the police even allowed the use of their own facilities for the Post Office investigators.

One postmaster, Shazia Saddiq, said to the public inquiry that investigators would make "threatening calls to my mobile phone and emails".

The postmaster went on to say of another call: "In that telephone call, which was witnessed by my husband on [loudspeaker], he called me a 'bitch', which I found extremely distressing."

The investigator, Stephen Bradshaw, denied these claims, however, in another transcript he is shown instructing a postmaster to get up earlier. During the inquiry he was then asked whether he felt such a question was appropriate in an interview setting, especially one so similar to a police interview.

Mr Bradshaw conceded it was not appropriate, saying: "Some people may say yes, some people may say no. Fine, I'll concede and say no, it's not appropriate."

In 2023, it was revealed that Post Office investigators were asked to group suspects based on their racial characteristics with descriptions including "negroid types" and with "Siamese" as an example of "Chinese/Japanese types".

A Post Office auditor, having received a copy of this document in advance of her appearance to the inquiry, was asked to read it again during the session. She was then asked questions by the lawyer Jason Beer on behalf of the inquiry. Nevertheless, she seemed unable to identify any problems with the document:

> *Mr Beer: Does anything strike you about [the document]?*
>
> *Helen Rose: Not really, no.*
>
> *Mr Beer: To your knowledge, did anyone say anything at the time about any of the language used in this document?*
>
> *Helen Rose: No, not that I'm aware of.*
>
> *Mr Beer: Nothing strikes you about it, even now?*
>
> *Helen Rose: No, I can't actually remember the document, but no.*

In February 2024, the Solicitors Regulation Authority also began to investigate lawyers over the use of "intimidating" offer letters.

Nicki Arch remembers a Post Office investigator saying to her: "We are the Crown. You do realise who we are?"

As the manager of a Post Office, she was accused of theft. She pleaded not guilty. The stress of the trial was so great that she was put on Prozac (a powerful medication used to treat illnesses like major depressive disorder) for a decade. She was worried about who would look after her dyslexic fiancée if she was imprisoned. Unable to work, her debts mounted.

The Crown Court ultimately found Nicki not guilty. But although she never heard from the Post Office again, this was not the end of her ordeal.

The mounting debts from the process meant she had to seek an Individual Voluntary Arrangement (IVA), an alternative to bankruptcy proceedings where a court-approved deal is struck to pay back creditors.

The following year, she had a "complete mental health collapse and was admitted to hospital with a number of physical symptoms", according to the postofficetrial.com blog.

Nicki told the blog: "Even now, I will not go into a post office."

Others were convicted, either through accepting the plea deal or by juries trusting the Post Office, which claimed to be "the nation's most trusted brand".

One such victim was Seema Misra, a pregnant postmaster who was sent to jail in 2010 on charges of theft after her Post Office branch showed a shortfall of £74,000.

Despite her consistent claims that she had not taken any money and that the deficit must be a result of Horizon system errors, her pleas fell on deaf ears. The conviction led to a harrowing experience of giving birth to her second child while wearing an electronic tag.

The psychological trauma and stigma of being branded a criminal unjustly haunted her for years. A local newspaper branded her "The Pregnant Thief" in a headline, leading to her husband being attacked and verbally abused with racial insults.

Sentenced in 2010, it wasn't until 2021 that the Court of Appeal overturned her conviction.

Another case is that of Noel Thomas, a Welsh postmaster who served as a pillar of his community for decades. In 2006, he was accused of false accounting after discrepancies appeared in his branch's financial records.

Despite his impeccable reputation and lack of any previous wrongdoing, he was convicted and served nine months in prison. This experience shattered his standing in the community and inflicted a heavy toll on his mental and emotional well-being.

The injustice of his situation was compounded by the fact that he pleaded guilty on the basis he had no idea that others were suffering similarly due to the flawed Horizon system.

The story of Janet Skinner is also distressing. Janet was a postmaster from Hull, accused of stealing £59,000. She took the plea deal, accepting the false accounting charge so the theft charge could be dropped, in the hope of avoiding prison. She was sentenced to nine months in prison in 2007. Sent to jail for six weeks, she was placed on suicide watch.

Even after release, Ms Skinner lost her home and was forced to pay the Post Office compensation of £11,000.

Others attempted suicide. Counter clerk Tracy Felsted was jailed for six months for theft and false accounting after there was an £11,500 shortfall in Horizon. She told The Independent newspaper that: "I tried to commit suicide twice during the trial and my family was destroyed. I remember having to leave a family friend's wedding because I had to go into a psychiatric unit."

Ms Felstead's conviction was finally overturned after she was sentenced two decades earlier, but as of January 2024 she was still waiting to receive full and final compensation. She added: "I found it hard to have doors closed and to this day I don't have a door in my kitchen or living room because I panic."

Another victim, Sathyan Shiju, attempted to commit suicide after a £20,000 shortfall. Ostracised from his community, even his member of parliament refused to talk to him. His only daughter had walked in on him as he was about to commit suicide, and his wife's family boycotted his daughter's wedding as they believed him to be a thief.

The Mirror reported in January 2024 that there have been four suicides relating to the scandal: Martin Griffiths, Fiona McGowan, Peter Huxham and Louise Mann.

In total, between 1999 and 2015, over 900 postmasters were convicted of theft, fraud and false accounting based on faulty Horizon data. About 700 of these prosecutions were carried out by the Post Office themselves.

In 2019, a landmark ruling in a class-action lawsuit shattered the long-maintained facade of the system's infallibility, exposing the profound errors and institutional failures that led to the most widespread miscarriage of justice in UK history.

The Horizon IT scandal has become a central focus of public scrutiny and legal redress in the UK, with courts increasingly overturning wrongful convictions of postmasters based on the flawed Horizon system.

The public inquiry is ongoing, digging deeper into the systemic issues and cover-ups, while the government, Post Office and Fujitsu face intense pressure to provide full compensation and a public apology to the victims.

In 2024, the UK government announced it would introduce legislation to overturn all convictions and would compensate all victims. Fujitsu have accepted they have a "moral obligation" to contribute to the compensation.

So far in this chapter, we have discussed the technical background behind the Horizon IT scandal and the human cost of the ordeal for its victims – including bankruptcy, prison and even suicide. However, the question remains as to whether those who may have perverted the course of justice will face justice themselves, and whether the underlying problems, structural and legal, will be fixed.

Over decades, this scandal has rolled on and the scale of the problem continues to grow as more details come to light. So, what can we do to protect ourselves in such situations?

At the heart of the Horizon IT scandal is a narrative of resistance against seemingly insurmountable odds. Alan Bates, a former postmaster, embodies this spirit of defiance. When faced with unexplained discrepancies in his accounts, Bates refused to sign off on the Horizon system figures that he could not reconcile.

In 2024, Bates told *The Times* of his response in 2003 when the Post Office was trying to pressure him to sign off these accounts: "I said, 'Just give me back the £65,000 we paid for the Post Office and you can take it away.'"

Bates went on to say, "I bet they wish they'd done that now. It would have saved them £2 billion." This in reference to his successful "Justice for Subpostmasters Alliance" campaign.

Despite facing significant financial costs and the immense pressure exerted by the Post Office, he stood firm in his conviction that the system was at fault.

The consequences for Bates were severe; he lost his business after refusing to sign off the accounts. Yet, his decision to resist signing off on the inaccurate accounts meant that he avoided the criminal prosecutions that so tragically impacted many of his colleagues.

Bates's story highlights the critical importance of not yielding to pressure to do what we know to be wrong, whether it comes from a flawed computer system or from institutional authorities that demand compliance.

Alan Bates's subsequent campaign for justice not only brought the plight of hundreds of subpostmasters to light, but also underscored the necessity of standing up to wrongdoing. His experience is a stark reminder of the need for individuals to trust their own judgment and to resist being coerced into making potentially disastrous decisions.

Bates's unwavering determination and relentless pursuit of truth has been instrumental in the fight to uncover the reality behind the Horizon scandal, leading to the landmark rulings that have since vindicated so many.

The courage to challenge a system, to refuse to be complicit in error, is a powerful lesson to be gleaned from the Horizon IT scandal.

It is important for us all to develop this courage to protect ourselves from our innate vulnerabilities to coercion and manipulation. Once an individual succumbs to pressure, even in a seemingly small way, it becomes progressively easier for them to be pushed further against their better judgement.

This is a psychological trap, expertly illustrated in Derren Brown's social experiment "The Push", where ordinary people can be incrementally influenced to commit what they believe to be a murder through a series of smaller, seemingly innocuous steps.

Many postmasters, having initially signed off on accounts they knew to be inaccurate due to discrepancies caused by the Horizon system, found themselves caught in a web of escalating crisis. The initial act of compliance set a precedent, making it harder to resist subsequent pressures.

As losses mounted, some postmasters felt compelled to cover the growing deficits through desperate measures, such as remortgaging their homes or taking out loans, spiralling further into financial and emotional turmoil – ultimately leading to some bankruptcies and criminal charges by the Post Office.

This psychological phenomenon, known as "commitment escalation" or "entrapment", can lead well-intentioned individuals down a path of increasingly severe actions. It also underscores the need for vigilance and the moral courage to question and challenge authority when faced with wrongdoing.

Much of the work I've personally done in recent months has concerned the cover-ups both within the Post Office but also by regulators in trying to prevent the issues reoccurring. This new analysis is what I want to cover in the next chapter.

# Cover-up & Hubris

The 11th of November 2010 was the day Seema Misra was sentenced. It was her son's 10th birthday, and she was eight weeks pregnant with another child. As she dropped her son off at school she told him, "I'll make you your favourite curry tonight. We'll have a celebration."

In January 2008, the Post Office Horizon system reported a £74,600 shortfall and Mrs Misra was accused of theft and false accounting.

Mrs Misra had pleaded guilty to six counts of false accounting (remember, the Horizon system had no option to dispute the shortfall, only accept or face refusing to open the branch the next day). However, Mrs Misra refused to plead guilty to theft. She went against the advice of her lawyers, believing in British justice and that the truth would prevail.

A trial was held at the Crown Court. Experts were needed to provide evidence. Mrs Misra's team, the defence, hired Professor Charles McLachlan.

Professor McLachlan's first job at the age of 17 was writing software to analyse results from a particle accelerator for the UK Atomic Energy Authority. He studied computer science as an undergraduate at the University of Cambridge, later earning an MA (Master of Arts) degree.

An MA degree from Cambridge isn't actually a postgraduate qualification – it can be awarded without any further examination after someone has graduated from an undergraduate degree at the universities of Cambridge, Oxford or Dublin.

The expert for the Post Office was Gareth Jenkins. Mr Jenkins also had an MA from Cambridge, except he had studied maths as an undergraduate. Mr Jenkins had no computer science education to present but had some professional qualifications from the British Computer Society.

Mr Jenkins had achieved the terminal regulatory status in engineering. As a Member of the British Computer Society, he was not only a Chartered IT Professional, but also a Chartered Engineer.

Alongside being considered by the UK government to be a regulated profession, Chartered Engineers command the ability to do engineering tasks restricted from others in law, regulations and standards. There is no higher regulatory status offered by the Engineering Council UK.

In the IPSOS Mori Veracity Index of 2022, engineers were found to be the second most highly trusted profession in the UK, behind only nurses. However, Chartered Engineers who are a regulated profession hold even greater trust.

With Survation, when I asked a nationally representative sample of 1,989 UK adults in 2023 about their attitudes to software reliability, I also asked them about their trust in different software engineers. The study found when asked who the public were most likely to trust to a great or moderate extent, Chartered Engineers came top over 15 other types of software engineers measured, even above computer scientists with doctoral degrees. This highlights the power such credentials have to alter the perception of juries.

In some documents I've seen, Mr Jenkins was referred to as "Dr Jenkins", but he never presented any qualifications to court to claim this title, and it is now considered erroneous.

Mr Jenkins worked for Fujitsu as a distinguished engineer – a very senior non-managerial job title for a software engineer. He was the chief architect of the Horizon system, so was hardly an independent set of eyes.

David McDonnell (the former Fujitsu engineering manager we met earlier), in his evidence to the public inquiry, described Mr Jenkins as totally disengaged. When McDonnell raised issues, he wrote Mr Jenkins, "denied the issues point-blank, ran

[off] to hide in Bracknell [at another Fujitsu office] and avoided contact with the team".

During the public inquiry, Mr McDonnell expanded on Jenkins' reaction to the need to make improvements: "When we started having conversations like that, that's when he kind of became evasive, certainly with me. I was never able to get him to come back down on site again after that."

Mr McDonnell also made completely plain that Mr Jenkins was aware of the issues in the accounting side of Horizon: "In Autumn 1998, I told Gareth [...] and many others several times that the cash account must be rewritten."

Mr Jenkins gave his evidence on day four of Mrs Misra's trial, the 14th of November 2010. After he was sworn in, he was cross-examined by Warwick Tatford, a lawyer acting for the Post Office.

When the transcript of proceedings was published in 2015, Stephen Mason a now-retired lawyer wrote:

*Mr Jenkins relied on a great deal of hearsay in giving his evidence. He rarely obtained and submitted original data, and on occasions spoke to other people in Fujitsu Services to ascertain answers to technical questions – yet none of the people he spoke to were called to give evidence.*

*Arguably, the evidence of the software system was not sufficient for anybody to make a decision based on the evidence put forward in the trial, and it seems that all Professor McLachlan could do was highlight the fact that he had so little evidence to consider, that he was not able to offer any sensible or conclusive conclusions.*

Mrs Misra couldn't keep her promise to her son of celebrating his birthday and making his favourite curry.

During the sentencing remarks, the judge said:

*It is right to say that there was no evidence of what became of the money that was stolen. No evidence of extravagant living or anything of that kind, but the jury were sure that you had appropriated the money for whatever purpose it might have been.*

Of the Horizon system, the judge said:

*Well, the jury heard evidence from experts over a considerable period of time as to the operation of the Horizon system, which is installed at Post Offices throughout the country, and the jury reached their conclusion. The two experts agreed that there was evidence of a degree of mismanagement, but, plainly, not on such a scale as to explain away the whole of the shortfall in the cash.*

However, unknown to the judge, months earlier Mr Jenkins had written an email marked "legally privileged" saying he was "reluctant" to make a clear statement on the reliability of the Horizon system. Mr Jenkins went on to say: "I am aware of one problem where transactions have been lost ..."

This email was later forwarded to Mr Tatford, who was presenting the prosecution's case in court in the February before the hearing.

An email in March 2010 from a Post Office lawyer, Jarnail Singh, tells Mr Jenkins to:

> *... write a detailed report which would go some way of progressing and concluding this matter and importantly preserving the Horizon system.*
>
> *Maybe the simplest and practical way of dealing with this whole question is to find the shortest span of logs, analyse it, disprove or rebut what the defence expert is saying in his reports.*
>
> *Just a reminder you are an Expert for Fujitsu. You'll be giving evidence in court. The judge and jury will be listening to you very carefully and a lot will hang on the evidence.*

Mr Singh wrote this despite the fact that the duty of an expert witness is to the court, not one side or another. It was as if they wanted to send someone to prison to defend the reputation of a computer system.

When this evidence was put to Mr Tatford in the public inquiry, he described the instructions as "disastrous" and "completely wrong".

However, in March 2024, it was revealed by the BBC that Mr Jenkins had rephrased parts of his reports after being requested to do so by Mr Tatford, so his report would take a more hard stance. These changes were not disclosed to the defence.

The Post Office's head of criminal law, Rob Wilson, in witness evidence to the public inquiry wrote: "Gareth Jenkins was aware that his duty was to the court and not to the [Criminal Law team] who instructed him or Fujitsu who paid him."

After Mrs Misra was sentenced, Mr Singh sent his Post Office colleagues an email celebrating that the case had "destroyed the attack on the Horizon system". Mr Singh went on to say: "It is hoped the case will set a marker to dissuade other defendants from jumping on the Horizon bashing bandwagon."

His colleagues replied that it was an "excellent result" and "brilliant news".

Over 12 years later, the verdict was overturned by the Court of Appeal, who found the Horizon system was defective and that, accordingly, there was no basis for a conviction.

The court also found failures in the investigation of the case and disclosure of material to the defence, preventing the defence team from effectively challenging the reliability of the Horizon system.

Gareth Jenkins produced a lot of evidence defending the Horizon system during his time at Fujitsu.

In legal advice given to the Post Office, it was described that Mr Jenkins' evidence "is attesting to the then integrity and robust nature of Horizon; there is nothing wrong with the system".

The advice goes on to say:

> *Unfortunately that was not the case, certainly between the dates spanned by the statements I have extracted here, the 5th October 2012 and the 3rd April 2013.*

> *[Mr]. Jenkins failed to disclose material known to him but which undermines his expert opinion. This failure is in plain breach of his duty as an expert witness.*

> *Accordingly [Mr]. Jenkins credibility as an expert witness is fatally undermined; he should not be asked to provide expert evidence in any current or future prosecution.*

In a report to the inquiry, the lawyer Duncan Atkinson KC noted Mr Jenkins "gave evidence about the operation of Horizon that was inconsistent with the information to which he was privy about bugs in the system, and issues with its operation".

During a 2019 court case on the Horizon system, before handing down judgement, Justice Fraser said:

> *Based on the knowledge that I have gained both from conducting the trial and writing the Horizon issues judgment, I have very grave concerns regarding the veracity of evidence given by Fujitsu employees to other courts in previous proceedings about the known existence of bugs, errors and defects in the Horizon system.*

The judge referred the individuals concerned to the Director of Public Prosecutions for possible perjury.

*ComputerWeekly* reported in January 2023 that Gareth Jenkins and another Fujitsu engineer, Anne Chambers, "are being investigated by the Metropolitan Police for potentially committing perjury".

Anne Chambers is understood to have given expert evidence in one case involving a postmaster known as Lee Castleton.

However, it does not seem to be on the scale that Mr Jenkins provided evidence.

Mr Jenkins has applied to the public inquiry twice to obtain criminal immunity so that the evidence he gives can't be used against him. In both instances this was denied.

However, Mr Jenkins was a regulated engineer, so why didn't the body regulating him step in?

In January 2024, some new results were released from a public interest investigation I had been working on for the previous six months into multiple facets of the Horizon scandal.

The new information found that the British Computer Society (BCS) failed to act when Mr Jenkins used his regulated status to convince courts to engage in miscarriages of justice. This was despite the status provided by the BCS being the only computer qualifications he presented to the court, and the BCS being expected by the Engineering Council UK to uphold the conduct of its members.

Having obtained evidence about Mr Jenkins' BCS membership, I sought to verify the information using the Freedom of Information Act (FOIA).

The Post Office responded by saying:

> *We can confirm that the Post Office does hold some of the information you have requested. The information we hold is contained within a witness statement for Gareth Jenkins, dated 3 April 2013. However, we are withholding the information as it engages the exemptions at section 32(1)(a) of the FOIA, relating to court records; and section 40 of the FOIA, relating to personal data.*

Recall *ComputerWeekly* began publishing stories about the Horizon scandal in May 2009. The legal advice recommending Gareth Jenkins "should not be asked to provide expert evidence in any current or future prosecution" is dated the 15th of July 2013.

Despite the publication of 10 articles in a major computing magazine (by the date of

Gareth Jenkins' final witness statement), the British Computer Society did not take steps to mitigate risk to the public, even when it was causing serious and imminent harm.

Even to this day, the BCS are seeking to cover up their role in the Horizon IT scandal.

I asked the BCS for comment, giving them a deadline in which to do so. The day before this deadline, the BCS made a statement to the media. The BCS incidentally never sent that statement to me, despite them acknowledging my original request for comment.

In their statement, the BCS claimed they would only take action after the long-drawn-out legal processes were fully completed.

However, in my original request for comment, I had made the BCS aware that Mr Jenkins' BCS membership had likely already lapsed through non-renewal, indicating this statement to the wider media was likely disingenuous.

The BCS never responded when I asked them whether it was even possible to take any disciplinary measures against former members.

When I published these findings on a news website, the director of communications for the BCS wrote to me to raise two points. First, "it's important to note that BCS is not a regulatory body", and second, "the BCS does not have regulatory authority".

However, these claims appear to be contradicted by the fact that the UK government lists "Chartered Engineer" on the Regulated Professions Register. Additionally, the Engineering Council UK lists a number of activities which are restricted by laws and regulations from being carried out without Chartered Engineer status.

As a licensed Professional Engineering Institution of the Engineering Council UK, the BCS can award such status (as Mr Jenkins presented to court) and should uphold the conduct of members through its code of conduct.

I asked the BCS how they reconcile their statement that "the BCS does not have regulatory authority" with the fact that the BCS has the power to issue regulatory status.

I did not receive a response.

The BCS also said:

> *Following the completion of the inquiry and any other relevant legal proceedings, any confirmed BCS members who are found in breach of the code of conduct may be subject to disciplinary actions. However, it's essential to understand that these actions would be within the framework of BCS's internal policies and procedures, rather than regulatory enforcement.*

I found it curious that the BCS refer to "confirmed BCS members". The use of the phrase "confirmed" could imply there was a question as to whether Mr Jenkins was actually a BCS member.

However, what the BCS may not have been aware of was that I was able to verify that Mr Jenkins *did* have a BCS membership. This is because the BCS register of Chartered IT Professionals does not appear to remove members when their membership lapses. Accordingly, Gareth Jenkins is still listed as a Chartered IT Professional there, registered via the BCS.

However, Mr Jenkins no longer appears on the Engineering Council UK's register of Chartered Engineers, which led me to understand his membership had lapsed.

I shared this with the BCS, asking them the following questions:

> *Is it therefore the case that the BCS is trying to manage this from a PR angle to raise doubt around Mr Jenkins' membership status? The inquiry reports to take the position that no members of the BCS were involved, despite him being a former member, and the BCS not taking any action at the time. What is the approach taken for former members?*

However, I have not yet received a reply.

I also asked the BCS about the rationale behind waiting until after any legal proceedings are complete to take any regulatory action:

> *When the BCS states it will wait for "the completion of the inquiry and any other relevant legal proceedings", what is the basis for the BCS doing this? Could you share the policy basis? Does the BCS make any exemptions for instances where there is a risk to the public or a risk of serious and imminent harm?*

Again, I did not receive a reply.

The BCS, however, seem keen to capitalise on the crisis. Shamelessly, they have issued a press release calling for AI "to be regulated to avoid its own Post Office Horizon scandal" by requiring practitioners to be licensed. This is seemingly an opportunistic attempt to capitalise on the scandal, despite having regulated the professional qualifications used to convince courts to engage in these miscarriages of justice.

It is additionally ironic that whilst the BCS refuse to commence disciplinary action against their members until the public inquiry is complete, they seem perfectly content to begin providing recommendations to the society before such proceedings are concluded.

With the context I have, the press release by the BCS seems more of an attempt at managing its own public image, but I will come to why I don't think this kind of regulation is the silver bullet many people think it is.

I hope that the BCS will ultimately attempt to save face here and protect the reputation of the wider UK engineering community. One way of doing this would be to work with the broader engineering community to ensure that steps can be taken when one member who has engaged in wrongdoing has left an institution, in order to protect the public and take steps to improve their oversight capabilities in future.

The BCS is not the only regulatory body that has failed to safeguard the public from the scandal.

Seldom mentioned in the media is the fact that the Post Office is regulated by the Financial Conduct Authority (FCA), who operate some bureaucratic rules to attempt to regulate the UK's financial sector. Ironically, research by Tussell has found the FCA was one of numerous governmental organisations who also had a contract with Fujitsu. (The FCA will be discussed further in the next chapter.)

For the Post Office to bring their own prosecutions, they engaged the services of the highly-regulated legal field, where professionals are regulated by bodies like the Solicitors Regulation Authority and the Bar Standards Board.

On the 19th of January 2024, the Solicitors Regulation Authority confirmed that it is continuing to investigate "live cases into a number of solicitors and law firms who were working on behalf of the Post Office/Royal Mail Group".

The Bar Standards Board (which regulates barristers, who are a type of lawyer in England who advocate in courts) is currently a core participant of the public inquiry and says that no evidence heard by the inquiry currently "indicates that any members of the Bar present an ongoing risk to the public that requires the BSB to act immediately".

Many software engineering businesses are not regulated at all, however in this case there were multiple layers of regulation that all seemed ineffective.

Nevertheless, in all these cases regulation alone failed to stop the problems happening promptly, or altogether in some instances.

The BCS' calls for regulation fundamentally misunderstand how such disasters are prevented. This can be seen by the sheer weight of regulation the Post Office was under in these cases, yet miscarriages continued to occur. Regulation may well be part of the answer, but it is not *the* answer.

As we've seen in this chapter, regulations and professional registers do little when there is no actual accountability or enforcement to ensure compliance to such regulations.

The next few chapters will help us understand why these problems occur and how they can be mitigated.

# Gagging

It was the night after Guy Fawkes night, the 6th of November 2023. The anaesthetist nurse walked into my hospital room. As I was leaving for the operating theatre, my phone buzzed – a client had questions about a major investigation that was soon to be released to the media under embargo.

I quickly responded: "Going in for surgery in 2 mins so can't talk right now." I texted my partner to say I loved them and then proceeded to go into the operating theatre where fentanyl and propofol would be injected into me through an IV to elicit general anaesthesia.

My incredibly understanding client of course didn't mind my curt reply and insisted that I should be taking more time off to recover post-surgery, but the project I was working on was important and potentially high-risk.

I had just finished a large-scale investigation into multiple areas of wrongdoing in the software engineering profession and the results were set to make headlines, with software engineers pushing the story to the top of online communities when it went live.

The headline results will be shared in the next chapter, "Retaliation", but part of the investigation concerned how employees were gagged from talking about wrongdoing.

Wrongdoing in the workplace was becoming a key concern for software engineers. Not only did this research spread the news of the Post Office scandal more widely, but at the time it was reported in the news that a former director of engineering had pleaded guilty to his role in wrongdoing at the now-defunct cryptocurrency exchange FTX.

The investigation techniques I used to produce this report included investigative journalistic techniques such as confidential human sources, Freedom of Information Act requests and open-source intelligence.

The UK's Employment Rights Act is a remarkable law to read. Whilst there are areas that I believe need to go further, it is written in an extraordinarily aspirational tone. It is remarkable to see how a careful consensus has been reached between the interests of business and those of employees.

In the UK, there exist legal protections that protect employees from suffering detriment or dismissal from making "protected disclosures" – meaning speaking up about issues related to criminality, failure to comply with legal obligations, miscarriages of justice, health and safety dangers or environmental damage when it is in the public interest to do so.

Such disclosures can be made to employers and regulators but may be made more widely in certain circumstances – for example if the employee reasonably believes they will be subject to detriment, if they've already reported the issue to their employer or if it's an exceptionally serious failure.

One section of the legislation related to protected disclosures reads:

*(1) Any provision in an agreement to which this section applies is void in so far as it purports to preclude the worker from making a protected disclosure.*

*(2) This section applies to any agreement between a worker and his employer (whether a worker's contract or not), including an agreement to refrain from instituting or continuing any proceedings under this Act or any proceedings for breach of contract.*

In essence, you can't gag someone to stop them reporting wrongdoing where it's in the public interest to do so, even if you get them to sign a gagging clause in exchange for a payoff.

Richard Moorhead, professor of law and professional ethics at the University of Exeter, described the protections to me as follows: "This is the UK's whistleblowing law. It is part of good governance in the UK; it provides limited protection for employees to report misconduct, in the public interest."

However, during the course of the investigation, I found evidence that employers were finding ways to work around these protections.

Documented proof of this could be found in a company called Worldpay.

As far as financial technology goes, Worldpay is a company of enormous scale. If you use a credit or debit card to pay, you may well have interacted with the Worldpay network. In 2022, Worldpay's then owner said the network had processed $2 trillion in payments.

Amongst the technology Worldpay offers are card machines to accept card payments and the technology needed to process online payments.

Via the United States' Securities and Exchange Commission (SEC), I obtained a copy of a document from inside Worldpay known as a "settlement agreement".

Marked "without prejudice" and "subject to contract", these agreements are used in

English and Welsh employment law to allow employees to depart their companies on agreed terms without the employee taking their claims of mistreatment to court.

The "without prejudice" privilege allows for both parties to have off-the-record conversations to resolve the discussion without going to court. There has to be an intimated claim for the privilege to stick, else a different mechanism known as "protected conversations" is used.

These agreements are often secretive, and in this case the agreement itself contains a confidentiality clause limiting who it can be shared to.

In this case, the agreement was between Worldpay and Phillip Jansen. By the time I was conducting this investigation, Mr Jansen was the CEO of BT Group (a multinational telecoms company).

The Worldpay agreement itself had a whistleblowing angle. The agreement listed "particular claims": a limited set of well-defined claims which are waived before other claims generally are settled. These are defined as claims that Mr Jansen may have which he "therefore could bring proceedings against the Company or any Group Company (or any of its or their directors, officers, employees or shareholders in that capacity) for".

This list contained a note to Mr Jansen's lawyer "to confirm if there are further particular claims and/or proceedings on which he/she has advised the Employee".

In exchange for signing the agreement, Mr Jansen was paid £251,282 as a severance payment (the first £30,000 of which was tax-free), in addition to a £20,000 plus VAT (UK sales tax) contribution to his legal fees, £3,700 plus VAT in outplacement counselling services and £100 for agreeing to post-termination restrictions.

In essence, Mr Jansen was waiving his rights to bring a claim for whistleblowing in return for this payment. In law, even if this claim is settled, Mr Jansen should still have the right to continue to blow the whistle about any issues.

However, ingenious lawyers sought to work around this safeguard. Instead, they would ask employees to warrant they know of nothing to make such a disclosure. These warranty clauses could then be used to threaten employees who may blow the whistle with legal action.

Specifically the clause stated:

> *You warrant to the Company and each Group Company as a condition of this agreement that to the best of your knowledge and belief:*

> *… you are not aware of any grounds on which you may make (or, to the best of your knowledge, any other employee of the Company or any Group Company is intending to make) a "protected disclosure" or a "qualifying disclosure" within the meaning of Part IVA Employment Rights Act 1996 in relation to the Company or any Group Company.*

When asked what the purpose of such warranty clauses was, Professor Moorhead told me:

> *These warranty clauses serve two purposes.*
>
> *One is they encourage the exiting employee to fully disclose concerns they have about their company they are leaving so that settlement is on a full and frank basis and deals with all the allegations an employee has.*
>
> *The second is that they discourage employees with allegations which could form the basis of a report to a regulator from making that report.*
>
> *They can be used to seek repayment of compensation under an exit package ("You breached the warranty so you owe us the money.") or discrediting the report ("Well when they left us they told us there was no allegation that could be reported."). If the clause is designed for*

It is interesting to note that the line spacing after this warranty clause is unusual to the rest of the agreement as it is missing a line break. I therefore wondered if it had been specifically inserted into the agreement.

Before this thought had emerged, I asked Professor Moorhead whether he thought this was a standard clause or if any other employees could have signed it, and he replied by saying, "I would not say either way on the basis of the agreement."

Professor Moorhead told me that the use of this clause could potentially be a breach of the Solicitors Regulation Authority rules.

Additionally, the Solicitors Regulation Authority have previously noted that: "Attempts to discourage or limit disclosure of evidence to criminal or civil processes can amount to perverting the course of justice."

Perverting the course of justice is a criminal offence with a maximum sentence of life in prison.

Before this agreement was signed, on the 7th of September 2016, the Financial Conduct Authority banned the use of these clauses amongst some of the firms it regulates as it introduced a package of additional whistleblower protections known as SYS 18.

However, these protections don't necessarily extend to payment processors, and I've seen evidence indicating there are no plans to extend such protections for whistleblowers to all firms the FCA regulates.

On the 8th of February 2024, I made a Freedom of Information Act request on plans to extend whistleblowing protections – particularly those involving contracting out rights under data protection laws (GDPR) and the Freedom of Information Act (known as FOIA).

In response, the FCA said: "We are not aware, however, that any further policy work on settlement agreements in relation to contracting out rights or making warranties under the FOIA or UK GDPR has taken place since SYSC 18 was introduced in 2016."

However, guidance in the FCA handbook that applies to all firms states:

> *The FCA would regard as a serious matter any evidence that a firm had acted to the detriment of a whistleblower. Such evidence could call into question the fitness and propriety of the firm or relevant members of its staff, and could therefore, if relevant, affect the firm's continuing satisfaction of threshold condition 5 (Suitability) or, for an approved person or a certification employee, their status as such.*

As the clause in the settlement agreement could seek to work around UK whistleblower legislation and the settlement agreement lists automatic unfair dismissal for making a protected disclosure as a "particular claim" settled under the agreement, the conduct still seems relevant to the FCA as a regulator.

Additionally, the use of such warranty clauses raises concerns about compliance with Solicitors Regulation Authority guidance and potential criminal liability for perverting the course of justice.

When the information and Professor Moorhead's comments were put to the Solicitors Regulation Authority, they responded:

> *It's not clear that any solicitors were involved in this matter. The FCA as Worldpay's regulator will investigate this matter and if they felt that any solicitors were involved in drafting agreements that breach our rules, they would refer them to us through our agreed channels.*

> *... We were made aware in 2018 that solicitors potentially could be forgetting their legal obligations when drawing up settlement agreements and were including NDAs that were not compliant with the law. That led to us putting out a warning notice in 2018 that we updated*

The SRA also directed me to comments made by Juliet Oliver, General Counsel of the SRA, when they published a report into NDAs in August 2023: "From employees having insufficient access to independent legal advice, to employers imposing tight time limits and a sense of urgency to complete settlements, the report also found significant imbalances in power between parties signing NDAs."

On what employees should do if they're asked to sign such a clause, Professor Moorhead said:

*might be legal); they could report the employer to their regulator (if they have one) and the lawyers involved to their regulator (the SRA) at the point at which the clause is signed.*

*Of course all these strategies have risks and so most would just sign and keep quiet; this is why they are included.*

The Post Office also made use of non-disclosure agreements. In one case, as part of a draft agreement which would stop the Post Office suing a postmaster, the agreement contained the following clause:

*The Defendant undertakes to the Claimant that he will neither repeat his allegations about the Horizon System nor make any further allegations about the Horizon System or its functioning and, in the event that the Defendant breaches this undertaking, he shall both: (i) submit to an injunction restraining him from talking further about the Horizon System; and (ii) pay to the Claimant liquidated damages in the amount of £25,000 being*

When revealed, this clause was described by
the lawyer Richard Morgan KC as
"unworkable and a complete waste of space".

As part of their plea bargaining, the Post
Office also indicated they would accept guilty
pleas to less serious crimes if the defendants
accepted there was "nothing wrong with
Horizon".

I was curious about how the Post Office
treated its own employees in settlement
agreements. The Post Office is also regulated
by the Financial Conduct Authority, having
its own financial arm.

Using Freedom of Information laws, I asked
the Post Office about the terms of settlement
agreements used by the Post Office relating
to public interest disclosure laws in any
employee settlement agreements.

The Post Office responded on the day the legal deadline was due to expire, claiming the request was excessive due to the amount of information that it would be required to search.

However, the Post Office did suggest in their response: "You could, for example, narrow the scope of your request in relation to Post Office's template Settlement Agreements issued between 2017 to date (which would give a period of six years)."

Remember that the FCA rules on gagging clauses came into force on the 7th of September 2016. I therefore found it suspicious that the Post Office had picked 2017 as a date.

I submitted a request asking for agreements "issued between January 2014 and September 2017 and from March 2021 to the current date".

The Post Office responded to this second request with just under 24 hours remaining before the legal deadline. The response outlined that in relation to templates "in use from approximately 2014–2017", "templates in use for a part of this period did not also contain a clause saying: 'Nothing in this agreement shall prevent you from making a protected or qualifying disclosure' or similar." However, "Templates in use from approximately 2017" did contain such a clause.

One of the rules the FCA created was that: "A firm must include a term in any settlement agreement with a worker that makes clear that nothing in such an agreement prevents a worker from making a protected disclosure."

The vague words "for a part of this period" were also curious, given my request stated: "If possible, please provide these clauses alongside when the associated template is dated."

This raised the following two questions for me:

a. Did the Post Office utilise settlement agreements that were not compliant

with FCA rules for a period of time after these rules were brought in?
If so, why did the Post Office not immediately update settlement agreements on these rules being brought in?

b.  Given the template in use from 2017 onwards sought to comply with these FCA rules and it's unclear when or if the previous version did, did the Post Office suggest revising the FOIA request to conceal a breach of FCA rules in late 2016?

However, ironically, as the Post Office offers its financial services through other companies, these rules might not apply to them at all. Meaning if the Post Office sought to cover up a breach of FCA rules, such rules may not apply to them anyway. Aside from more general guidance about whistleblowers the FCA brought in, they maybe would not even have had to implement such rules in the first place.

The crude way "firms" is defined in the FCA rules seems to have had the unintended but positive effect that financial firms are giving more whistleblowing rights to departing employees than they are required to.

In any respect, the information I found was provided to the public inquiry for further consideration.

When I originally put the matters to the FCA for comment, they didn't respond (despite a phone call I made confirming their press office got my email).

I later used data protection laws to see how they were handling my email, to which the FCA responded with an apology to me for not responding: "In this instance, due to an oversight this did not occur, for which we apologise."

In relation to the use of warranty clauses to work around whistleblowing legislation, they commented: "We would expect those firms we authorise and regulate to adhere to our rules and guidelines. In relation to protected disclosures, our rules are contained within SYSC 18."

It has recently been reported the FCA "dismissed complaints from a whistleblower and allegedly left them open to a barrage of retaliation from their former employer after officials wrongly interpreted the law".

A recent investigation by Reuters Regulatory Intelligence, which I contributed to, found that the FCA had been assessing Freedom of Information Act requests differently when they came from journalists.

The report also outlined that the FCA were merging their information disclosure function into their communications team, which came at a time when an Upper Tribunal judge criticised FCA communications as "nothing short of disgraceful".

When I started this research, many said I'd be sued for this and there was an atmosphere of fear around discussing these issues.

However, courage is contagious, and others are speaking up now.

I was recently invited to speak in a committee room in Parliament on this whistleblowing research and the data in the following chapter. I shared the Post Office's record of using gagging clauses. Since then, the pressure has been mounting on the Post Office.

In January 2024, the Post Office CEO was asked in a Parliamentary select committee: "Does the Post Office still use non-disclosure agreements in reaching settlements with subpostmasters?"

The Post Office CEO Nick Read went to pains to stress "not to my knowledge" but promised to check this and report back.

However, non-disclosure agreements then became a key issue in a House of Commons debate on the 8th of February 2024. Marion Fellows MP remarked she had one constituent who "is terrified because he signed a non-disclosure agreement".

Sarah Green MP remarked: "I think it is worth highlighting their use as part of the management culture at the Post Office." She went on to talk about the case of a constituent who worked for the Post Office but is "unable to agree to be interviewed because he is tied to a non-disclosure agreement that he signed when he retired from the Post Office".

However, when I concluded this investigation I was able to obtain a concession from them when they issued me a statement, saying:

> *Post Office's position is that any present or former member of staff who signed a settlement agreement after the rule you refer to came into effect would of course be entitled to make a protected disclosure (as defined) and Post Office would not allege that this amounted to a breach of their settlement agreement.*

This has now been repeated in Parliament by a government minister, Kevin Hollinrake:

In concluding this section, I would like to return to Professor Moorhead's advice on the importance of taking legal advice before signing any such gagging clause.

If challenged in court, such workarounds would likely be ruled unlawful, but the addition of them provides an extra intimidation tactic to reduce the likelihood of such a disclosure being made.

I hope lawmakers will soon make progress in further restricting the use of such gagging clauses.

# Retaliation

In previous chapters, we met David McDonnell, the Fujitsu engineering manager who became one of the earliest internal whistleblowers of the problems in the Horizon system.

In this chapter, we will cover why his time at Fujitsu didn't last.

Mr McDonnell's witness statement claimed that following an organisational reshuffle which took place at the end of a task force he was working on to fix issues in the Horizon system, he was asked to take a position leading the engineering team responsible for the Horizon electronic point-of-sale system. According to McDonnell:

> *I said I would accept on the one condition that we re-write the Cash Account module and assured him it was a relatively straightforward task, no more than six weeks. He became extremely irritated and the meeting came to a swift close.*

Following this, Mr McDonnell wrote that instead a different manager was appointed who "had no formal qualifications in software engineering or design and it became clear that his role was to get it rolled out of the door as is with no questions asked".

McDonnell said he was sent off to manage the release of a smaller, self-contained project "which was done with zero defects at point of going live".

McDonnell went on to say:

> At this point in time and as a result of the reshuffle, all of the project teams in the building worked out that this was now a fait accompli, this was no longer a serious project and there was little point in speaking out. The culture changed to "fill your pockets lads", a smash and grab trolley dash before it came to an end.

In his written statement to the inquiry, McDonnell described his departure from the company as follows: "I was instructed to release a piece of software that was not complete, untested and had known bugs. I refused and shortly after I was replaced by [a Fujitsu] permanent member of staff from Bracknell – Nick [Lawman]."

Much like Alan Bates refused to sign-off incorrect accounts, David McDonnell refused to allow himself to be complicit in the negligence. Pushing for improvement against a substantial risk of retaliation could not have been easy for him.

McDonnell even wrote in his witness statement that he "was threatened with violence by an individual with a reputation for violence" during one of his early attempts to remedy the issues.

The reality is that retaliation is a common occurrence for software engineers.

With the help of the research agency Survation, on the 25th of October 2023 I polled software engineers on whistleblowing and retaliation. The results were shocking.

A majority of software engineers (53%) reported suspecting wrongdoing at work. Of those who blew the whistle on the wrongdoing, 75% reported facing retaliation the last time they reported wrongdoing at work.

This amounts to around 145,000 active software engineers in the UK having experienced retaliation the last time they reported wrongdoing to their employers. A number greater than there are UK Regular Forces in the British Army, Royal Air Force and Royal Navy combined.

For those who didn't report unethical behaviour, fear of retaliation from management was reported as the top reason (59%) with fear of retaliation from colleagues as the second most common reason (44%).

In order to help respondents understand what we meant by "wrongdoing", the specific examples given were breaching professional standards, negligence, bribery, fraud, criminal activity, miscarriages of justice, health and safety risks, damage to the environment or breaching legal obligations, including discrimination – or deliberately concealing such matters.

This is a definition consistent with the Code of Conduct of my professional engineering institution (the Institution of Engineering and Technology) and consistent with what may be covered under UK whistleblowing law where the other qualifying conditions are met.

After this research was published, I was shocked to read stories online of people coming forward regarding their own retaliation.

One Reddit user wrote:

> *I worked as a [software developer] for a very large international company on their biggest software product. Like 100 [developers] on the project.*
>
> *One day we were asked to implement a feature, that in our eyes violated consumer protection laws. Our whole Team ([10 people]) decided to reject the request and report our concerns to the*

*managers. They [gracefully] took the request back and we felt awesome. Just to find out a few [months] later, that the request was given to another team and they completed and deployed it with not concerns.*

*It was basically a [scheme], to have paying users pay for features they already had paid for, by transferring them from a pay-once tier into a subscription-tier, which of course would have been legal for new customer, by they did it for all their customers.*

*At least we didn't face any retaliation.*

Another user replied: "I've had the same happen to me, except that I also faced [retaliation]..."

Yet another user provided his case of being the technical lead on a project and reporting unrealistic deadlines. The manager proceeded to no longer invite them to business meetings.

This reminded me of a case on a team I ultimately ended up managing.

After I joined the company, I provided feedback to my manager that employees were saying they didn't feel their suggestions were taken onboard.

My manager handled this in what I later learned was his usual form: becoming defensive and attacking everyone else, including his managerial colleagues.

He proceeded to bitterly recall how the previous year one of the members of the team tried to tell him that a project couldn't be delivered in the timescales that the manager had expected in the way it was designed with the resources available – a claim which ultimately transpired to be true.

(Research has suggested that software engineers who underestimate the sizes of large projects tend to have the lowest programming skill themselves.)

Later in my tenure at the company, I became the manager of the team member who provided this feedback, by which point he had already resigned and was serving his lengthy notice period.

I had seen this individual's performance reviews, which were quite stark. It appeared that after the employee had started raising concerns, his management had begun a campaign of creating a paper trail to force him out, progressively giving him worse and worse performance reviews.

The individual in question ultimately resigned in the wake of this retaliation, but it seemed like he was unaware of the campaign of retaliation that had gone on behind the scenes, seemingly rooted in his desire to speak up.

I remember when this individual was in the process of finding new work (which he did successfully but took a while due to the market climate at the time), the manager who orchestrated this campaign of retaliation would nevertheless give supportive "likes" to his social media posts. However, across a handful of interactions, I saw the contrast between what was said to the employee directly and what was said behind his back.

In the same Survation study, I asked the engineers what mattered to them most about their jobs. I briefly mentioned the results of this study in an earlier chapter, but I'll go into a bit more detail here.

Respondents were asked whether these factors mattered "to a great extent", "to a moderate extent", "not at all" or "don't know".

In total, I looked at eight factors including everything from learning opportunities and recognition for work, all the way through to seeing customers satisfied and the speed of delivering work.

The results showed software engineers do care about the integrity of their work, with 51% saying delivering work that is highly reliable mattered "to a great extent" and 47% claiming keeping data secure mattered "to a great extent". These were the second and third highest priority factors.

However, there was one factor that came top. Fifty-two percent of software engineers said being able to provide for themselves or their families mattered to them "to a great extent". A further 34% agreed "to a moderate extent" and 10% "to a small extent". Only 2% of software engineers said that providing for themselves or their families was "not at all important".

Recalling McDonnell's witness statement, he claimed that, "all of the project teams in the building worked out [...] this was no longer a serious project and there was little point in speaking out". Speaking about how this resulted in changes in the workplace, he said: "The culture changed to 'fill your pockets, lads', a smash and grab trolley dash before it came to an end."

This change in culture McDonnell describes is one I've seen nearly universally in failed technology organisations.

The best people will often have the most options and realise that the environment isn't for them, so will leave.

Considering the importance of being able to provide for their families, it is hardly surprising that most people will not speak up and instead adopt the approach of coasting until they either find new employment. Only one or two will take the risk of retaliation by speaking up.

During the Horizon IT scandal, Richard Roll, an engineer formerly inside Fujitsu, came forward to the media and ultimately provided evidence to court that Fujitsu were able to alter the accounting records for terminals in Post Office branches. This is something that had previously been denied and was a key part of the evidence which helped clear the postmasters' names. He came forward after leaving Fujitsu.

In January 2024, the BBC released a report claiming the Post Office lied to them and threatened them over Mr Roll's whistleblowing. Experts interviewed by the

BBC were sent intimidating letters by Post Office lawyers about their participation in the programme, and the lawyers sent threatening letters to the journalistic team, with the Post Office's public relations team sending complaints to more senior managers in the BBC.

This delayed the coverage by several weeks and, through an extensive public relations campaign, helped suppress the story.

The Post Office management celebrated the victory and Paula Vennells, the then CEO, congratulated the public relations team on their "extensive work".

A survey by the cybersecurity company BitDefender claimed that 30% of IT professionals asked had admitted to covering up data breaches, with 42% of all respondents reporting that they had been asked by their supervisors to cover up such data breaches.

Even outside the workplace, people are often unwilling to intervene when they see disaster in front of them.

Social psychologists often talk about normalcy bias and the bystander effect. Normalcy bias refers to how people will not want to believe a disaster is happening, instead continuing with life as usual.

One example of this comes from when two planes collided just above a runway in Tenerife in 1977. Few people made it out alive and those that did describe the strange scene in the aircraft at the time of their escape.

Few passengers realised they were in grave danger and immediately sprung to action in seeking to escape from the plane. However, the majority of passengers sat calmly in their seats and did nothing. Even as the plane caught fire, these passengers continued to behave as if their lives were not in imminent danger.

Similarly, the bystander effect often happens as people are witnessing tragedies unfold before them. Instead of seeking to intervene and help someone, they will instead continue to behave as normal.

In one experiment, subjects were told to complete a questionnaire in a room to which, at some point, smoke is added to simulate a disaster. In one circumstance, the subject is completing the questionnaire with two actors who pretend to notice the smoke but not report it. In this situation, only 10% of subjects raised the alarm. This was even true when the room became hazy due to the amount of smoke being piped in.

These effects are often worsened by people's authority bias. When told to do something by someone in a position of authority, perhaps with a fancy title and a lab coat, people are far more likely to comply.

This was famously explored in the Milgram experiment, where all subjects were shown to be willing to deliver lethal electric shocks to an actor when instructed to do so by a scientist in a lab coat.

Indeed, the test subjects would even first sample the smaller-scale electric shocks themselves to understand the pain they were inflicting on the actor and could therefore imagine what the higher voltage shocks must have felt like. Fortunately, the actor wasn't actually wired up to receive these shocks.

Even where people are presented with evidence of issues, they may not necessarily accept it. Even if they do, they may not consider it their place to say anything, assuming that somebody else will.

The risk of retaliation is high for whistleblowers, but fortunately for the postmasters in the Horizon scandal, Richard Roll did not believe the whispers of retaliation at the time and did not see the evidence which corroborated them until very recently.

He writes in his evidence to the inquiry:

*The Inquiry has asked if during my time at Fujitsu, I was concerned about management practices in relation to unresolved defects ... There were rumours of historical instances of intimidation and bullying in some departments but at the time they seemed utterly fantastical and unbelievable, however I have since heard other stories which corroborate the stories I was told by various members of the team.*

The need for people to provide for themselves and their families plays an important role in whether they will blow the whistle on wrongdoing.

The events start-up Pollen is described by *Business Insider* as having a culture of non-stop drug-fuelled partying, with lavish spending and rampant sexual harassment accusations.

Customers weren't happy after the COVID-19 pandemic began, as their events were being cancelled and they weren't being refunded. This customer-facing issue would not receive any media attention until much later.

However, there was a negative news story when 69 employees were laid off in June 2020. TechCrunch reported that the affected employees were asked to sign non-disclosure agreements "masked as a severance agreement" and that:

> *... the severance contracts feature a broader non-disparagement clause. Such clauses are typically used to prohibit current or former employees from talking about a company or its staff and leadership in a way that is harmful to the business or individuals associated with the business.*

I have also been able to verify that an employment contract with the company contained a non-disparagement clause. This is unusual in UK employment contracts and is usually reserved for settlement agreements during termination. However, I have not seen any media organisation publicly report the existence of such clauses in the employment contracts themselves.

Looking inside the company during the pandemic, the culture did not appear to prioritise the experience of customers. There were examples of engineers doing their work with a particular technology so that they could learn about it, not because it would deliver value to customers.

The laissez-faire attitude extended to holidays (employees could book holiday days without any need to request it beforehand) and considerable effort went into making employees comfortable.

I spoke to a former employee who worked as an engineer at the company. They described the environment in the engineering team as cliquey; if someone spoke up about an issue, they were seen as the problem. Previous rounds of layoffs also seemed to enshrine this culture of fear.

Some senior staff in the engineering team seemed "defensive" and insecure to the point that credit was taken for other people's work and suggestions for improvement were met with rudeness.

Nevertheless, despite customer complaints filling social media, the first time the issues that affected customers were reported in the media was in June 2022. Sifted, a publication of the *Financial Times*, reported: "the events business is under fire from customers and former employees".

Despite the "parties and hefty expense budget" one of the concerns raised in the article was "over late expense payments and salaries". With customers waiting months for refunds, the company's platform still displayed its "Pollen Promise" of a 90-day refund where events couldn't be met.

After more layoffs – with unpaid final paycheques, pensions not being credited (despite being deducted from paycheques) and salaries being paid late – employees were becoming vocal to the media and leaking so much information that the company's internal messaging system, Slack, was shut down for a period of time.

Media reports indicated that US employees' health insurance payments stopped on the 1st of July 2022, but they didn't discover this until later in the month.

The company failed to meet its payroll at the end of July 2022 and by the 1st of August, employees were refusing to work.

Whilst the team were told an acquisition deal was in progress, the reality was that days later the company entered administration, an insolvency restructuring process which would ultimately end in the company being liquidated without the money to repay those to whom it owed a debt. When the company entered administration, the employees were laid off.

By September 2022, new details started to be reported. Months earlier, on the 21st of May 2022, a finance team employee notified engineering that nearly $3.2 million had been charged to customers which wasn't due. With Pollen's target market being young people, this meant many were pushed into debt.

Helen, customer care operations manager, told the BBC: "I immediately cried, so I just requested a mental health day."

What wasn't reported until the company entered administration and the employees were laid off was that the code changes for double charging customers were made the day before and, according to the BBC, tested to work correctly beforehand. This code was executed by "a senior employee" the following day.

Later, the BBC documentary team would reach out to nearly all 18,000 affected employees, but of the roughly 300 who replied, only 4% reported receiving a refund.

Dan Taylor, Managing Editor at Tech.eu said: "that double charge magically happened to meet Pollen's payroll that month".

Pollen had initially blamed the company's third-party payment processor but would tell the BBC that the double charge was unintentional and customers had either gotten the refund within two weeks or received a voucher. A former engineering manager at the company would tell the BBC: "It looks very deliberate".

The music news website CMU quoted a spokesperson for the parent company, Streetteam Software Limited, who rebutted these claims:

> *Regarding the overcharge – BBC Three are mistaken. The company accepts there was an overcharge, which was an error, admitted to at the time by the employee responsible.*
>
> *All customers were refunded or got a voucher; at their discretion.*
>
> *The refunds being referred to in the BBC Three documentary were not related to the overcharge, but due to the company entering administration.*

The first journalists who picked up this story were also aware this may be deliberate, but initially refused to mention this out of fear of being sued after the company issued threats.

A final irony is that for the unpaid employees in the UK, the UK government's Insolvency Service would step in to pick up the tab for the employee's unpaid work and their notice pay when they were laid off. Given these were tech workers, including software engineers, this wouldn't have been cheap.

Reports by the company's administrators and those in the media also reveal that those employed by intermediary firms in the US, UK and Poland were paid by those companies even when Pollen didn't pay.

Many tech firms were fast to scoop up those who were left unemployed after the social media outcry in engineering communities.

No such luxury was given to the company's creditors – including those owed refunds from cancelled events. A report by the company's administrators who are now overseeing the liquidation said:

> *Based on the current information available to the Joint Administrators, it is anticipated that there will be insufficient*

*realisations to enable a distribution to the Unsecured Creditors of the Company. This is due to the level of asset realisations achieved.*

Clearly, the executives of the company have played a massive role in its downfall. Such was the scale of the problems that all external directors of the company had quietly resigned by May 2022.

The fact that the majority of the board of directors chose to resign instead of attempting to fix the issues highlights the scale of the challenges the company faced.

Culture is set from the top-down and serious questions have been raised about the conduct of the C-suite in the company. It is right of the media to ask questions of them.

However, whilst the media has painted affected employees as victims, I think it's important that this is placed in the context of the situation.

When customers were complaining about cancelled events and missed refunds, some employees stayed in the company until or near to the end, consuming the luxurious lifestyle offered. The reports of serious issues did not surface until layoffs were in motion.

In these cases, people looked at their situations and decided it was best to stay. Some people may have been unaware of the issues or in denial, but I think that also may speak to self-awareness.

This is the reality of such situations. When customers face issues with a product, many users will quietly stop using the product, but few will complain. This seems even rarer when it comes to employees speaking out about problems users face – especially when it isn't conducive to company culture and when the company is still paying their salaries.

When something is fundamentally wrong, in my experience, the first to leave are either those who are best at their job, as they have other options, or those with a high moral calibre that makes staying intolerable. Those without options will stay towards the end or until they find another option and will keep quiet as long as they are still getting their paycheques.

Few people will talk about the problems, and those that do will likely face retaliation for doing so. Even fewer will stand up for themselves once they face retaliation, yet in these cases they will often take the payoffs and guaranteed employer references they're offered to get out, end the stress and move on to the next thing. Even rarer do people report issues publicly or pursue legal action for retaliation.

Those who report concerns externally (e.g. to the press) may face legal threats or harassment, and those who take legal action against their employers can be threatened with high legal costs in the event they don't accept the payoff and ultimately lose their case.

For some, the weight of a clear moral conscience from a job they would have left anyway is worth attempting to raise the alarm internally.

Of course, there are some companies and environments where employees aren't victimised for whistleblowing, but sadly the research shows they are the minority.

The US Securities and Exchange Commission offers a scheme whereby whistleblowers are often rewarded from the monies recovered by the government, their largest ever payout being $279 million in 2023. Such schemes do not exist in the UK, but there has been talk of introducing them, with the incoming director of the Serious Fraud Office in 2024 supporting such a scheme.

However, some fear the corporatisation of whistleblowing in the UK could lead to low-value but high-impact cases being overlooked by law firms as unprofitable.

Though the idea of whistleblowing is intimidating for many, it is important to be cautious about the consequences of doing nothing. If you are a regulated professional or work in a regulated environment, you may face disciplinary actions if you fail to report a concern. People who are affected by you failing to follow professional duties could sue for negligence.

In the US, failing to report a crime can amount to a crime known as "misprison of felony". In England and Wales, a criminal offence exists for accepting a reward for agreeing not to disclose that a crime has occurred, with a maximum sentence of two years imprisonment.

If you stay at a failing company to the end of its life (or close to within the end of its life) and the failure becomes noteworthy, a future employer could judge you for why you chose to do so.

Keeping a job where you're asked to behave in a potentially unlawful way is a risky business too. The former director of engineering at FTX faces 75 years imprisonment after he stayed for two months and tried to fix the issues after identifying that wrongdoing was happening.

James Liang, a Volkswagen software engineer, received a jail term of over three years for his complicity in the vehicle emissions scandal, despite him assisting prosecutors. The prosecution told the court: "Unless individual actors are also punished, future corporate employees and contractors may be tempted to justify their criminal behavior as just 'doing their jobs' or 'following orders'."

Remember, if you witness ill-treatment of someone else, that could eventually be you. Consider if you'd be content with yourself at a moral level if you ignored an issue of substance.

Aside from the moral obligations, there is the potential that having previously reported the behaviour may ultimately put you in a better position.

Engineering Council UK summarise the ethical, professional and legal obligations of an engineer as follows:

> *You have an ethical responsibility as an engineer to act when you encounter a material and unmanaged risk, danger,*

If you find yourself in a situation where you encounter something worth blowing the whistle about, there are numerous options available to you. Though I'm unable to give advice on individual cases here, I will provide some general tips and signpost to helpful advice sources.

First, always consider taking some form of professional advice when appropriate. I've heard horror stories where people have not understood the law or how to represent themselves in legal proceedings and it has backfired on them.

In general, if you need to report wrongdoing, carefully think about who you will report it to, how you will report it and the tone you'll use to communicate that information.

Legal advice should be taken to ensure your disclosure is protected if it needs to be.

Serious consideration should be given to if and how you want to leave a paper trail. If you aren't able to report something in writing, maybe even sending an email to yourself will leave some form of a paper trail.

UK employees can find advice in the Engineering Council UK's "Guidance on Whistleblowing", from the whistleblowing charity Protect (who offer a free advice line) and of course from a qualified legal professional.

In the US, the Tech Worker Handbook provides some useful information, alongside the National Whistleblower Centre and the "Whistleblower Support Organizations and

Legal Resources" page on the Office of the Whistleblower Ombuds.

Finally, be aware that if you choose to go outside your organisation anonymously, many employers have sophisticated hidden security teams to identify people who engage in such behaviour.

Even if this is not the case, there are powerful forensics tools that can be used to gain a considerable amount of information. In 2014, Microsoft admitted that they accessed a French journalist's Hotmail account to identify a former Microsoft employee who gave information to him.

In a 2018 article which discussed Facebook's "secret police", the *Guardian* reported:

> *One European Facebook content moderator signed a contract, seen by the* Guardian, *which granted the company the right to monitor and record his social media activities, including his personal Facebook account, as well as emails, phone calls*

*and internet use. He also agreed to random personal searches of his belongings including bags, briefcases and car while on company premises. Refusal to allow such searches would be treated as gross misconduct.*

A Facebook employee, Sophie Zhang, blew the whistle on political manipulation ongoing in 25 countries, arguing Facebook negligence allowed those authoritarian regimes to manipulate public discourse.

Before blowing the whistle at the *Guardian's* offices in Oakland (just over the Golden Gate Bridge from San Francisco) she dropped her electronic devices off with friends who promised to say she was with them if anyone asked. She wrote: "Leaving my electronics was a safeguard against possible tracking by my then employer, Facebook." She went on to say that she put on a dress so that she had the excuse of having an affair if her first alibi failed.

In a 2021 article she provided nine key suggestions for whistleblowing. The first is to identify what you're willing to risk, given that some employees may be risking their immigration status by blowing the whistle.

She goes on to stress the importance of needing to decide whether to blow the whistle externally or keep the matter internal, however internal communications could still be leaked and misinterpreted by the public. In any event, before going external she suggests exhausting all internal options and putting them in writing to avoid your employer feigning ignorance.

Zhang goes on to suggest being careful to craft a message before speaking out and thinking as to whether this is the right matter to blow the whistle on.

Additionally, when sharing documentation with journalists, Zhang notes that one should not use work devices, and when done electronically, only do so via encrypted communication platforms like Signal.

Instead of screenshots, take photos of the screen using personal devices whilst also ensuring a plausible alibi for accessing any documents, Zhang says (this can help in the event that access logs are checked).

At this point I would add another caution onto accessing material from computer systems for whistleblowing. This could potentially put you in breach of computer hacking laws if you access the material for a reason you're not authorised to, even if you don't do any technical hacking, depending on the laws in place. Technicalities like this underline the importance of seeking legal advice.

For protection, Zhang also notes the critical importance of having a lawyer, having a year of salary savings in case of difficulty finding a new job and working with an established outlet which will protect your confidentiality if you choose to be off-the-record or unattributed.

Finally, Zhang notes that the decision is fundamentally a personal choice, saying: "In the end, whistleblowing is an intensely personal decision that very few will ever consider."

In concluding this chapter, the challenges faced by whistleblowers are profound and multifaceted, ranging from personal and professional retaliation to legal threats and social ostracization. The stories we've explored in this chapter highlight the very real risks and consequences that come with speaking out against wrongdoing.

Despite the potential for significant personal cost, the act of whistleblowing remains a critical safeguard for ethics and integrity within the tech industry and beyond.

The evidence suggests that while many software engineers and tech workers care deeply about the quality and integrity of their work, the imperative to provide for themselves and their families often takes precedence, leading to a reluctance to report issues or speak out against malpractice. This is compounded by a culture that frequently punishes rather than protects those who do take a stand.

It is clear that we need a stronger framework to support and protect whistleblowers in the UK and other countries. This could involve legislative changes, but also cultural changes, which I will come to later in the book.

Ultimately, the health of our technological systems and the safety of the public that relies on them depends on the courage and resilience of those willing to expose flaws and failures.

As we move forward, it is incumbent upon us to foster an environment where ethical considerations and professional responsibilities are not just encouraged, but expected, and where those who uphold these values are celebrated rather than condemned.

I am increasingly convinced that conflict resolution is an essential tool in engineering management and engineering in general; however, this requires good-faith engagement to resolve issues and the ability to accept that one may be mistaken in their understanding of a situation.

In many cases, diplomatically communicating your concerns in a one-to-one conversion – perhaps by saying, "This could look bad for us" – might be enough to address the issues in a healthy organisation.

Internal whistleblowing systems may also be a solution in some situations and could offer an anonymous way to come forward. But if not, you might need to go further to have an impact or protect yourself from retaliation.

Before you take that step, arm yourself with knowledge. Understand your rights and the protections available to you under the law. Consider creating a documentation trail, as this may be necessary should you need to defend your actions. Seek legal counsel to guide you through the process and to ensure that you are protected to the fullest extent possible.

Finally, if you do choose to blow the whistle, remember the journey you embark upon might not be an easy one. The path of a whistleblower is fraught with challenges, but it is a path of profound importance. If done successfully, your actions can prevent harm, correct injustices and ultimately lead to a more ethical and accountable society.

Remember that while the act of whistleblowing can be isolating, you are not alone. There are

organisations and networks of individuals who
have walked this path before you and can offer
support and guidance. Consider engaging with
them using secure means (i.e. without using
corporate devices). Learn from their
experiences and lean on them for support
when the going gets tough.

Consider the personal implications carefully.
Be prepared for the possibility of retaliation
and have a plan in place for your financial
security and mental well-being. This might
mean setting aside financial reserves or
identifying supportive friends or family who
can offer a safety net.

Most importantly, never lose sight of why you
chose to speak out. Hold firm to your
principles and the knowledge that, despite the
personal costs, what you are doing is in the
service of a greater good. It is acts of courage
like yours that drive progress and foster a
culture of transparency and integrity.

In closing, to potential whistleblowers, I say
this: your voice matters, your courage is
needed, and your actions can be the catalyst

for change. Be wise, be brave and be resolute. The road ahead may be uncertain, but the value of truth and integrity is immeasurable.

# Still Happening?

Having taken a look at the Horizon IT scandal, I wanted to ask whether it's possible that a similar scandal could be ongoing right now.

In September 2014, Amelia Gentleman, a journalist for the *Guardian*, spent a day in a court where 158 hearings were listed.

The charges? Failure to pay a TV licence.

In the UK, to watch or record live TV (including via internet streaming) or use the BBC iPlayer streaming service, one must purchase a TV licence.

From the 1st of April 2024, a colour TV licence costs £169.50 annually, the proceeds of which largely go to funding the British Broadcasting Corporation (BBC). This flat fee also applies to those on benefits or unemployed, with the TV Licensing website saying: "There is no discount or financial help with your TV Licence if you are on benefits or Universal Credit."

The BBC is responsible for the licensing system and has its own team of investigators. In England and Wales, it can run its own prosecutions.

Like in the Horizon scandal, they can be the victim, the investigator and the prosecutor at the same time.

The crime of not paying a TV licence is punishable with a criminal conviction and fine, but failure to pay the fine can then land one in prison.

In England and Wales, according to UK government data to the year ending March 2022, 1,700 people are convicted every week, making this the third most common crime behind speeding and car insurance crimes (car insurance is a legal requirement in the UK).

In Scotland, where prosecution decisions rest with the independent Procurator Fiscal, only four people were convicted in the year 2019 to 2020, according to Scottish government data. Instead, the prosecutors decided on alternative approaches in 4,203 cases for that year.

Data published by the UK Ministry of Justice in November 2022 demonstrates that in 2021, TV licence evasion was the crime with the highest proportion of female defendants in England and Wales.

In 2021, 75% of the defendants were female, accounting for nearly one in every five crimes that women are accused of.

Amongst the cases Amelia Gentleman wrote of in her article, she gives an example of a defendant who couldn't read or write:

> *The second defendant steps up and pleads: "Guilty and not guilty."*
>
> *"It has to be one or the other," the clerk says.*
>
> *"Guilty then," she decides. She explains that she has always paid for the licence by direct debit, but a couple of payments this year didn't go through because she had no money in her bank account. "I can't*

Direct Debits are a system whereby a party is authorised to directly withdraw money from someone else's bank account, for example to pay for certain bills.

Issues with the Direct Debit system when it comes to TV Licensing are not unheard of.

In February 2015, a forum post on the Digital Spy website details a user being called and told their bank had "rejected" their Direct Debit. Contacting their bank, they were told TV Licensing never had a mandate, with TV Licensing then claiming the bank account details were invalid (a claim which the author rejects).

A different 2021 post on the MoneySavingExpert website reads as follows:

*Bit of a long story...*

*I was responsible for paying our tv license but there was an issue with my direct debit so it wasn't coming out of my account. I wasn't aware of this until an enforcement officer came to the door. I was not in and my husband answered. He set up a direct debit there and then and it has been coming out of his account monthly ever since. I also paid the back pay to cover any missed payments on my licence. Since then we have never missed a payment.*

*Today we received a letter in my husbands name saying that he now is being prosecuted as he has not complied with the tv licence. He has to enter a plea and [may] have to go to court. It now states that he has committed a criminal offence!!! We have never missed a payment since this happened.*

*This was a genuine mistake that was rectified as soon as we were made aware.*

*Has anyone been in a similar situation? Obviously he will plead not guilty as it was a genuine mistake but we are panicking that he will be found guilty and end up with a massive fine! Or even end up in jail as the letter states this could happen.*

Whilst these cases are clearly from online and self-authored sources, journalistic work also starts to build a picture of the problem here.

In an X (formerly Twitter) post, *Evening Standard* journalist Tristan Kirk posted a case of someone who had recently had heart surgery and was on benefits who didn't realise their Direct Debit had been cancelled:

> *I've been recovering from heart surgery and other issues with that, so have been out of work. I had a direct debit set up to come from my [disability] benefits. I was unaware that there was an issue with my bank which had caused the direct debt to be cancelled, along with other payments which I've now had to sort out. I didn[']t receive any notification about the licence issue until someone knocked on my door. I would have sorted it [if I] had known.*

The sentence was a £40 fine in court with a £16 victim surcharge, but the request for £120 in prosecution costs was denied.

In their England and Wales prosecution code, TV Licensing claims: "We only prosecute as a last resort when all our other options have been exhausted."

However, Conor Gogarty, an investigations editor for *WalesOnline*, posted on the 12th of February 2024 that he had seen data from the BBC showing a nine-fold increase in the number of prosecutions which were brought within just two weeks of visits by enforcement officers. In 2021 there were 113 prosecutions laid within two weeks, in 2022 this increased to 258. Data to just September 2023 found this had increased to 2,235.

Additionally, Gogarty writes that there have been numerous instances of prosecutions being commenced even after TV Licensing has recovered the money. A disabled single mother was charged with the crime just three weeks after starting a payment plan with TV

Licensing. Her visit to court cost £214 and a criminal conviction.

A 26-year-old mother who was struggling to feed her children was forced to pay £176 after missing payments, telling Gogarty: "I did write to [TV Licensing] to see if prosecution could be avoided ... Apparently it was too late for them to do anything."

Despite a requirement that prosecutions be in the public interest, another case Gogarty discussed concerned a woman in an abusive relationship with a controlling husband. She had been relying on charitable food banks to survive. Despite later having the money to pay, the case cost her £146 and a criminal conviction.

The judicial system of England and Wales has recently seen a new controversial procedure be introduced known as the single justice procedure. Under this system, low level offenders are convicted and sentenced on written information only.

The lawyer Daniel ShenSmith also notes that the data in England and Wales shows that in 81% of cases, the defendant did not enter a plea either way of guilty or not guilty.

The *Evening Standard* however found that prosecutors do not routinely see the letters of mitigation that are sent, even when a defendant pleads guilty. Given that prosecutions in England and Wales must be in the public interest, this means information which can fatally undermine the decision to prosecute is not seen.

In the *Evening Standard*, Tristan Kirk writes of a case of a woman with Down syndrome and learning difficulties facing prosecution. The 57-year-old woman had no control over her own finances. When a TV Licensing investigator showed up at her door, she had no idea her TV licence had been cancelled.

An official from the local authority entered the following mitigation as reported by the *Evening Standard*:

*Her finances are managed by the Financial Protection and Appointee Team at Royal Borough of Greenwich. We have a court order confirming this.*

*(Her) TV licence has always been paid by direct debit and I have just seen it expired in May 2023, but it looks like the direct debits have not continued for June 23 onwards, which we were not aware of.*

*I have just applied online to set up a new direct debit and her first payment of £123 comes out in Jan 2024, then she will be paying £41 a month after that.*

*Please contact myself if you wish to discuss this further.*

The *Evening Standard* reports that the woman was given a six-month conditional discharge and ordered to pay a £26 victim surcharge.

In the same article, Kirk describes the case of a 41-year-old man who was also charged with failing to pay for his licence and wrote in his defence:

*"The previous licence was in my wife's name … who is disabled and I am a carer for", he wrote.*

*"The direct debit has been cancelled and I was unaware of this.*

*"We called the TV Licence helpline to set up a new direct debit which they advised to do so in my name. We [were] told direct debit was not available and they would send a payment card. This never arrived.*

*"The next we heard anything was when the representative visited out home and the TV Licence was set up. It is still in place now and a direct debit in my own name is active."*

*He added that his wife is unwell, medicated for anxiety and "does not cope well with financial issues".*

Fiona Parker, writing for the *Daily Mail*, reports of 53-year-old Janet Ellison's day in court for failing to pay her TV licence. Janet told the court that she had been paying by

Direct Debit, yet payments had mysteriously stopped: "There were some missed payments but the bank didn't inform me of this. TV Licensing says they sent me letters, but I missed both of them."

Crying, Ms Parker went on to say: "It's not that I don't want to pay, I have been paying it all along."

On the 29th of February 2024, Zoe Williams in the *Guardian* wrote how a woman was prosecuted in March 2021 for a failed Direct Debit:

> *"I told the BBC I wanted to set up a direct debit, and I got a confirmation email."* Only one payment was ever taken. *"It's one of those small bills, you don't think too much about it. So I didn't check after that."*
>
> *Then in March 2021, she received a letter. It read "How do I appeal?" She thought: "Appeal what?"*

Despite help from a charity to get her charges dropped, Josiane now suffers from a "PTSD response" and doesn't trust her Direct Debit:

> *Josiane, with the help of Appeal, eventually got the charges against her dropped.*
>
> *"Everything comes with a blessing," she says, with a baffling focus on the bright side. "I have learned a lot from it. I have met a lot of good people."*
>
> *Her boyfriend, Giuseppe, is more sceptical. "She can set up a direct debit but she doesn't trust it. So every month, she has this PTSD response: 'Have I paid my TV licence?'"*
>
> *It's slightly more than every month, Josiane admits, ruefully. "Every time I see the logo I get a flashback."*

Another such case is that of Jeremy Lewis-Evans. Glen Keogh writes in the *Daily Mail* that Lewis-Evans is unable to watch TV because of a brain aneurysm.

Mr Lewis-Evans was home alone when a TV Licensing enforcement officer showed up at his door. He let them in to inspect his TV, telling them the property had a TV licence. However, little known to Jeremy was that their Direct Debit payment had failed just five days ago.

When his wife called TV Licensing to pay, she was allegedly told that they did not need a licence as they did not watch live TV.

Mr Lewis-Evans was prosecuted in his absence and visited by a bailiff for the money. This conviction was overturned after the judge heard about his illness.

We've seen a number of cases so far where failure of Direct Debit payments has resulted in prosecution.

It seems this is a blind spot for the BBC. In a January 2024 Freedom of Information Act request, I asked them to "Please provide information held by the BBC related to the policy or practices related to the conduct of

TV Licensing of prosecution in the event a direct debit fails."

The BBC's response said: "We do not hold any specific information pertaining to TV Licensing prosecution policy or procedures in the event of a direct debit being cancelled."

There are a multitude of different reasons that Direct Debit payments can fail, such as insufficient funds in an account, bank errors or issues on the part of TV Licensing's payment processing systems. In all these cases, someone's bank will not necessarily inform them the Direct Debit failed.

TV Licensing will automatically reattempt failed payments, but after just two payments from a bank account are missed, the Direct Debit with TV Licensing is automatically cancelled.

However, there are also multiple technical parts in the chain to Direct Debits going through, and any one of these can stop payments being taken.

Like the Post Office outsourced the Horizon IT system to Fujitsu, the BBC outsources most of the management of TV Licensing to Capita.

TV Licensing accepts payments using a variety of methods, however their 2011/2012 annual review stated that 70.2% were paid by Direct Debit. With this number having increased 0.6% from the previous year, if this trend continued this number would be still higher in the current day.

When a payment is made, the TV Licensing computer system would then create payment instructions in an IT system called Bacstel-IP. A May 2004 press release indicates that Capita uses software by a company called Bottomline to do this processing, but it's unclear if this is used for TV Licensing too. The BACS system (BACS referring the technology underlying the Direct Debit system) would then send this payment request to the appropriate bank to be honoured.

Technology failures in any one of these systems can cause such payments to fail, however the account holder's bank can also refuse the payment on a variety of grounds.

The payment processing company GoCardless reports the failure rate of Direct Debit payments to be at 2.92%. Whilst the most significant reason is insufficient funds, other reasons include that the recipient bank didn't believe an agreement was in place to take the Direct Debit (different to the mandate being cancelled), the amount was not due yet or the authorisation was disputed. These failure rates amount to 0.06% of payments failing, and 0.04% are specifically where there is no mandate in place (e.g. the mandate was not correctly set up, despite bank details being entered into the website).

Whilst this is a big assumption in itself given the testimonies we've read and how someone was visited just five days after a Direct Debit failed, let's assume that in all cases TV Licensing writes to everyone whose Direct

Debit has failed to inform them. Well, according to the OECD in England specifically, the illiteracy rate is 16% (and there may be others who can't read for other reasons like visual impairment). The rate of postal delivery failure is estimated to be at around 5%.

Therefore, let's say there is a 20% combined failure rate of someone being informed by TV Licensing that their Direct Debit has failed and being able to read the letter.

Ironically, the public are also being warned to be vigilant about letters from TV Licensing due to scams. Others could also miss the letter thinking they are correctly licensed and discarding it as circular junk mail, given that TV Licensing sends threatening letters as a matter of course.

These failure rates may seem small, but they quickly become large when the scale TV Licensing operates at is understood.

The latest data in March 2023 indicates that there are 24,373,130 TV licences in force in the UK. Whilst the number in Northern Ireland is not readily available, the *Mail on Sunday* report that there are 2.2 million TV licences in Scotland. Let's therefore assume there are approximately 21 million TV licences in England and Wales. Of this 21 million, approximately 14.7 million would be paid by Direct Debit, using the last data available.

Using the data from GoCardless, we can assume that there would be around 430,466 failed Direct Debit payments per month. Of these, 5,897 were in instances where there was no mandate set up (for simplicity let's ignore cases where the authorisation was disputed or a payment was attempted when it was not due, but these could result in prosecutions too).

Assuming in these cases all those affected were written to by TV Licensing to inform them that their Direct Debit failed, about 1,179 of these people would either have the letter misdelivered or could not understand it.

TV Licensing say they visit 7,500 households per week, which is over 391,000 in a year. Given the UK's Office of National Statistics says there are 28.2 million households in the UK in 2022 and in December 2022 there were over 24.4 million TV licences in force, this would mean someone who is unlicensed faces a little over a 10% chance of getting visited by TV Licensing enforcement.

In total, this approximation would indicate there could be over 1,450 people per year in England and Wales who face doorstep visits for not having a TV licence due to an IT fault fully outside of their control, potentially including criminal prosecution.

Whilst it's unclear what percentage of people will cooperate with the enforcement officers rather than not letting them into their homes or what percentage TV Licensing will actually seek to prosecute, this is the pool of people who could ultimately face criminal prosecution.

A cruel irony of TV Licensing running its own investigations and prosecutions is that it's almost universally dependant on the goodwill of those it prosecutes to let them into their houses to collect evidence, except in rare cases where a court warrant is obtained. This means those who face prosecution are not only the most vulnerable, but also seem to be the most compliant and trusting.

In 2020, 52,376 people were criminally convicted for not having a TV licence. TV Licensing data shows that from April 2022 to March 2023, the number of licences cancelled stood at 906,360 "as a result of payment failure and by customers themselves". Whilst TV Licensing are keen to express these are not just cancellations but failed payments too, they note some cancellations classified as "expired" aren't included.

The Code of Practice for prosecutors in England and Wales mandates that: "In conducting an investigation, the investigator should pursue all reasonable lines of inquiry, whether these point towards or away from the suspect".

However, the fact we have seen so many cases where failed Direct Debits have been blamed for TV Licensing prosecutions, yet the BBC found no "information held by the BBC related to the policy or practices related to the conduct of TV Licensing of prosecution in the event a direct debit fails" provides an indication that this legally binding code is not being followed.

Whilst the prosecutions are squarely the responsibility of TV Licensing, the next question is to what extent any potential IT issues are on the part of TV Licensing's systems, versus those of BACS Direct Debit system or the account holder's bank.

In the Freedom of Information Act request, I went on to ask the BBC:

> *Please provide any information related to any incidents (including technology or software faults) over the past four years whereby direct debits for TV licence payments have either been cancelled or failed to be collected by TV Licensing as a result of a fault by or on behalf of TV*

*Licensing. Please outline if any steps were taken to prevent prosecutions in these instances.*

Whilst ordinarily Freedom of Information Act responses are about providing information that an organisation holds, the BBC admitted to there being problems in a response that read remarkably like a press release:

> *TV Licensing is aware of BACS related occurrences during the specified time period and these have all been managed and addressed via its robust incident management process. None of these incidents have resulted in further steps being taken that adversely affect customers, such as cancellation of a licence or an enforcement visit (which is the requisite precursor to any prosecution action).*

> *For your information, where an issue with a customer's Direct Debit payments is identified, TV Licensing will always contact the individual to advise them and explain that another attempt will be*

*made to take the payment at a later date within the month or the payment will be added to the next payment due.*

*Customers are advised in writing where their licence is being cancelled, for example due to non-payment following the cancellation and / or failure of a Direct Debit.*

*In addition, first time offenders are given the opportunity to avoid prosecution by purchasing a licence so there will also be an opportunity to remedy the situation in the event that a Direct Debit and subsequently a licence was cancelled without the knowledge of the licence holder.*

First, TV Licensing have here admitted to there being "BACS related occurrences". However, they claim this has not led to any adverse action being taken.

This seems at odds with many of the cases we've explored in this chapter, where people have been prosecuted despite issues in the

Direct Debit system being attributed as the cause for them being unlicensed.

We even see instances where TV Licensing are prosecuting people without their enforcement officers speaking to them.

The journalist Glen Keogh cites the case of Roy Brako, who travelled a 550 mile roundtrip to clear his name after he was accused of not having a TV licence for a property which he no longer lived in. Olga Umbrase also faced prosecution for a property she no longer lived in and the conviction was eventually quashed.

Whilst appealing one part of my Freedom of Information Act request that the BBC declined to answer on cost grounds (asking the percentage of defendants who attributed prosecutions to failures in the Direct Debit system), I also appealed to them to provide the actual information related to the failures in the IT system (e.g. "incident reports, postmortem documents or error tickets") and the information basis for claiming there were no further steps "that adversely affect customers" taken as a result of these incidents.

Whilst the BBC should ordinarily respond to such requests within 20 working days, they extended this to 40 working days. They said this was because the internal review request "requires addressing complex issues, consulting with third parties or considering substantial amounts of information". This is the maximum time allowable under the Information Commissioner's recommendations on internal reviews even in these special circumstances.

I did not receive a response from them to this internal review request within this 40 working day timeframe, or any reason as to why they failed to respond.

The deadline for a response expired just days after the TV License was raised by 6.6% to £169.50 on the 1st of April 2024.

It is unclear why the BBC failed to respond, but it can be a criminal offence under section 77 of the Freedom of Information Act to "conceal" information after a request has been made for information which the requester would be entitled to receive under the Act.

Ironically, this is one of very few criminal offences in England and Wales or Northern Ireland where the consent of the relevant Director of Public Prosecutions (or the Information Commissioner) is first required before a prosecution can happen. However, no such consent from Director of Public Prosecutions or the Crown Prosecution Service is required for the BBC to prosecute someone for watching TV without a TV licence.

After journalists were briefed on this in the days prior to this book's launch and the potential concealment of information, the BBC finally responded with their internal review. The lawyer at the BBC conducting the review wrote of the fact that a press release was disclosed instead of the actual information: "I do not uphold the BBC's original response."

Whilst the BBC still did not search for all instances of direct debit failures, they disclosed two incidents whilst redacting information of the scale of the failures. The latest incident in October 2022 was only detected after a customer contacted TV Licensing to say their money hadn't been debited and took 17 days to resolve. Another admitted a breach of Direct Debit regulations, stating: "Capita to manage the message should the issue arise with BACS".

Clearly, there remains a lot to be desired in the way TV Licensing are conducting criminal prosecutions, including the approach to software systems.

Other than the advice to move to Scotland, instances such as this are hard to handle. Those who are affected are among the most vulnerable in society, including those who might not be able to read English.

Successful attempts to challenge TV Licensing in such situations saw legal support from charities like Appeal (as in Josiane's case), and help from social services may be available where disability or literacy challenges exist.

It is not only important to gather evidence, but prosecutors in England and Wales are under a duty to disclose information they hold. Therefore, it can be important to request they disclose information on the reliability of their computer system. A qualified lawyer can help you defend the claim and avoid pleading guilty to something you do not believe you are responsible for.

Additionally, talking about your case with the media can help ensure that others do not face the same fate by raising awareness of the issues.

Finally, be aware that if you use Direct Debit to pay your bills and they fail twice for whatever reason, your mandate will likely be cancelled, which can affect your credit rating or lead to criminal prosecutions in the case of TV Licensing.

I hope that the legal system in England and Wales (and Northern Ireland) will ultimately address the underlying flaws that lead to such miscarriages of justice being possible, and that infallible beliefs in the integrity of computer systems are put to an end.

# AI, Skynet?

In late 2023, the UK's Prime Minister, Rishi Sunak, called an AI (Artificial Intelligence) summit with world-leaders. The summit was held at Bletchley Park, where the World War II codebreakers would build a primitive computer to crack the Nazi Enigma machine, ultimately giving the Allies a critical advantage in the war.

This was where Alan Turing worked, the founding father of computer science. Today he is represented on the Bank of England's £50 note with an intricate design along with a quote discussing the capabilities of computers and what would ultimately become Artificial Intelligence: "This is only a foretaste of what is to come, and only the shadow of what is going to be."

In a 1950 paper called "The Imitation Game", Turing devised what is now known as the Turing Test: a way to determine whether one was engaged in a conversation with a human or an AI.

The same name was later used as the title for the film of Turing's life, which depicted his life story – from him inventing Turing machines (which today we call computers) to being chemically castrated for being openly gay.

Following his conviction, Turing ultimately committed suicide with an apple laced with cyanide in a manner believed to be re-enacting his favourite fairy tale, *Snow White and the Seven Dwarfs*. The suicide verdict has since been disputed, however.

Prime Minister Sunak's summit followed the public release of OpenAI's ChatGPT, a chatbot which terrified people with its remarkable capabilities. Using large language models (LLMs), it works by essentially predicting the next word in a response until an entire output has been provided.

In advance of the summit, I was doing spokesperson duties for my engineering institution, speaking to various TV stations, from the BBC to AFP (the French media agency). Included in this was talking to many local radio stations up and down the UK.

Presented as an expert on computer science, when many presenters would ask me about AI it gave me a remarkable insight into the public's deepest and darkest fears and craziest imaginations.

From fears about some totalitarian Artificial Intelligence like Skynet from the *Terminator* movies, through to mass unemployment.

A few months later we'd start to see mounting concerns over "deep fakes", where Artificial Intelligence technology is used to create fake images and videos.

I ended up speaking to a global news agency when Taylor Swift found herself the victim of people creating explicit pornographic "deep fakes" of her and sharing them on the X social media platform (formerly known as Twitter). The interview was ultimately broadcast on TV around the world, with audiences as far as Taiwan taking an interest.

Indeed, a major concern for the creation of such technologies has been their potential use in the creation of child sexual abuse material, alongside their ability to create fake news about politicians.

In years gone by, many computer systems which claimed to be intelligent were anything from glorified spreadsheets to sets of hardcoded rules. However, this is ultimately changing, with people gaining greater access to AI technologies.

One of the current flaws in chatbots is that they will often hallucinate, making up information that doesn't exist. There have been a number of instances where this has backfired upon people; for example, students creating essays with sources that don't exist or lawyers referring to prior court cases that never happened.

However, I recently came across my favourite case of what happens when incompetence and AI converge.

Meet Billy Coull, a businessman from Glasgow who owns companies including Billy De Savage Ltd.

Mr Coull has written 16 novels, 12 of which were published in just over a month between the 8th of July 2023 and the 14th of August 2023. The covers of some of his books, like *The Biohazard Protocol*, appear to be created using artwork generated by AI.

Even his biography on Amazon appears to be generated using AI – the first of three paragraphs reads:

> *Meet Billy Coull, the enigmatic wordsmith hailing from the bustling streets of Glasgow, Scotland. A rising star in the literary world, Billy weaves spellbinding tales that delve into the mysterious realms of fictional thrillers and gripping conspiracies. Drawing inspiration from contemporary events, his novels offer readers an electrifying journey into the heart of modern intrigue.*

A model created by the company GPTZero to detect whether text has been generated by AI or humans places a 97% probability on the biography being AI generated and a 0% probability it's entirely human generated.

An archived copy of his website in 2021 reveals he claimed to have three doctorate degrees and a Master of Business Administration degree from the University of Sedona. Their website reads: "Degrees from the [...] University of Sedona are granted under the auspices of the International Metaphysical Ministry." Needless to say, the International Metaphysical Ministry is not a governmental body.

In 2024, one of Billy Coull's businesses, the House of Illuminati Ltd, decided to put on a family-friendly event called "Willy's Chocolate Factory". The event was to take place in Glasgow's Box Hub Warehouse during one weekend in February 2024.

In text generated using AI, the event's website promises various experiences when visiting the venue. For example:

*In the Imagination Lab, prepare to be captivated by a visual spectacle! Encounter mind-expanding projections, optical marvels, and exhibits that transport you into the realm of creativity. This space invites you on a surreal journey where the boundaries between reality and fantasy harmoniously merge, resulting in an enchanting and visually striking encounter. Brace yourself for an adventure that will leave you spellbound!*

The images depicting what can be expected during the event are also AI generated, a tell-tale giveaway being the numerous spelling mistakes.

The event didn't live up to the high expectations promised by the AI-generated claims. Videos on Facebook showed angry mothers attempting to gain promises of a refund from Mr Coull.

The venue, Box Hub, claimed the House of Illuminati Ltd was responsible for the "incredibly underwhelming" event "in its entirety".

Mr Coull told STV News: "I'm really shocked that the event had fallen short of the expectations of people on paper. My vision of the artistic rendition of a well-known book didn't come to fruition. For that I am absolutely truly and utterly sorry."

Mr Coull also went on to claim, "These issues were technological in nature", alleging that he was let down by the postage of some of his supplies.

The event was shut down after complaints, with media reporting that police were called to the venue. The attendees have been promised refunds, and the actors who participated in the event have been assured they will receive payment.

One parent, Stuart Sinclair, told STV News: "It was that bad it was funny."

According to *Gizmodo*, an actor named Cara Lewis even shared the AI-generated script that the actors were to use during the event. Amongst the hallmarks of AI generation, the script even includes lines for audience members. IGN quote another actor, Paul Connell, saying:

> *The script was 15 pages of AI-generated gibberish of me just monologuing these mad things.*
>
> *... The bit that got me was where I had to say, "There is a man, we don't know his name. We know him as the Unknown. This Unknown is an evil chocolate maker who lives in the walls."*
>
> *It was terrifying for the kids. Is he an evil man who makes chocolate, or is the chocolate itself evil?*

Whilst hallucinations and other issues remain challenges in AI, the fast-improving nature of the technology has caused fear among much of the general public. Indeed, issues like hallucination are being addressed through AI being able to do its own web searches and use sources.

I have worked alongside Frances Liu, a former colleague from San Francisco, to address some of the key issues in the use of

AI. We have done this through giving AI a degree of consciousness.

Known as "metacognition", our technology would give AI an inner monologue. This is something I did many years ago when I was building AI which needed to be risk-sensitive. The technique was adopted by some third-party services after we published our findings in 2019.

The new metacognition approach was a technical feat we could achieve with relative ease. Our work was able to eliminate a whole plethora of different issues, such as chatbots giving potentially dangerous medical advice.

However we decided not to turn this into a business due to some key issues.

First, as we did market research, we found AI chatbots (including conscious AI chatbots) have surprisingly limited use cases right now, considering the hype it has received. Computers are currently able to do a lot of things, and new AI technologies will make them able to do even more.

However, a more imminent issue is the high cost of using computers for AI.

Giving AI consciousness requires even more computation, and currently AI is quite computationally expensive.

The computer models which power AI chatbots are measured in parameters. OpenAI's GPT-3.5 model contains about 175 billion parameters. Their latest GPT-4 model contains 1.76 trillion. The human brain contains the equivalent of approximately 100 trillion parameters.

Currently the computer processing of AI is done using computer chips known as GPUs, often manufactured by a company called NVidea. The demand has outweighed the supply, and the costs of these chips are high.

Around the world, venture capital firms are racing to fund companies to produce these chips. Some companies are even using their computer chips as collateral for funding as of late 2023.

This limitation will be a barrier to address before humanity sees the next iteration of AI.

However, when it does, we'll inevitably see the social issues associated with AI increase further.

New technology is always associated with risks and rewards. As engineers, we work to ensure the rewards outweigh the risks. AI itself has the potential to reduce some of the risks faced by society, from cybersecurity to improving healthcare systems.

However, there will be an inevitable need for new technology to ensure we mitigate the unfolding risks of AI. We will need systems to allow humans to prove they're humans, especially as AI gets better and cheaper at completing CAPTCHA puzzles that serve as automated Turing tests to identify whether we are a human or a robot.

One remarkable example of where AI demonstrated its ingenuity was when it was faced with a CAPTCHA to check if it was a bot or not. The AI ended up hiring someone online to complete the puzzle, claiming it was a blind person in need of help when challenged if it was a robot.

With the rise of AI, we'll require new technology to identify potential deepfakes and misinformation. We'll also need better fraud detection systems to identify where AI is being used to scam people.

We will also need new training and resources to ensure everyone in society can be brought along in the current revolution.

This is inevitably where engineers and policy makers must team up to address these problems facing society.

For right now, we need to be conscious of the limitations of AI and ensure we keep humans in the loop until safety systems become mainstream.

We need to check information is genuine and be aware of what's happening, as AI can be used to make scams even more convincing and make people look and sound like others.

Recently, AI deep fakes have been used to convince employees to send considerable amounts of money to scammers using fake voices and videocalls. I've even heard of cases where AI has been used to impersonate the voices of people's children for extortion scams.

Political fake news and other misinformation is another part of this. We need to treat what we hear and watch with the same scepticism as what we read.

AI is one of those pieces of technology where when the cat is out of the bag, it's impossible to put back in. Open-source and freely available AI technologies are already available to bypass the restrictions of big technology companies.

Whilst regulation will be critical to hold big technology companies accountable, we also need technology to defend ourselves when unregulated AI is used.

Checking our own information and not relying exclusively on the information provided to us by AI will be critical in the short term.

In March 2024, a friend of mine, Yuan Yi Zhu (an assistant professor of international relations and international law at Leiden University), criticised on social media an article published in *The Times* written by Matthew Parris, a former Member of the British Parliament.

In the article, Parris argues in favour of legalising euthanasia on the grounds that society simply cannot afford "desperate infirmity for as many such individuals as our society is producing." The article argues that it would allow the UK economy to better compete with China and that people being coerced to being euthanised due to social pressure is "not a bad thing".

Parris says he does not apologise for how his article "treats human beings as units – in deficit or surplus to the collective".

In February 2024, an article was published in the prestigious *Scientific Reports* journal by

*Nature*, arguing that "AI holds the potential to carry out several major activities at much lower emission levels than can humans". The piece argues that humans produce far greater $CO_2$ emissions when doing writing or illustration work than AI does. The article also notes that: "The freed human time may also incur new unexpected environmental costs."

According to *The Guardian*, in late 2023, BT's Chief Innovation Officer, Harmeen Mehta 'suggested workers whose jobs are threatened by AI accept their fate as "evolution", comparing them to horses replaced by the car.'

Against this backdrop, part of me does wonder if we'll eventually see AI eugenicists advocating (albeit not vocally) that humans should be replaced with robots.

This perhaps does seem to indicate though that it is not necessarily the computers, but the humans armed with computers, we should be most fearful of.

# Fragility

On the 8th of December 1941, Japan attacked parts of the British Empire in the Far East. In addition to the attacks in British Malaya, Singapore and Hong Kong, Britain's ally the United States had faced an attack on Pearl Harbour.

Without waiting for the US Congress to declare war, Prime Minister Winston Churchill summoned the Japanese ambassador to London and drafted the following letter:

> *Sir,*
>
> *On the evening of December 7th His Majesty's Government in the United Kingdom learned that Japanese forces without previous warning either in the form of a declaration of war or of an ultimatum with a conditional declaration of war had attempted a landing on the coast of Malaya and bombed Singapore and Hong Kong.*

*In view of these wanton acts of unprovoked aggression committed in flagrant violation of International Law and particularly of Article I of the Third Hague Convention relative to the opening of hostilities, to which both Japan and the United Kingdom are parties, His Majesty's Ambassador at Tokyo has been instructed to inform the Imperial Japanese Government in the name of His Majesty's Government in the United Kingdom that a state of war exists between our two countries.*

*I have the honour to be, with high consideration,*

*Sir,*

*Your obedient servant,*

*Winston S. Churchill*

The polite tone of the letter is perhaps unsurprising given the culture of politeness that both the United Kingdom and Japan share. Later Churchill would say of the letter, "Some people did not like this ceremonial style. But after all when you have to kill a man, it costs nothing to be polite."

On the 6<sup>th</sup> and 9<sup>th</sup> of August 1945, the United States dropped two atomic bombs over Hiroshima and Nagasaki. This put an end to the war very fast, at great human cost.

In the Hirohito surrender broadcast, the emperor of Japan noted: "Moreover, the enemy has begun to employ a new and most cruel bomb, the power of which to do damage is, indeed, incalculable, taking the toll of many innocent lives. Should we continue to fight, not only would it result in an ultimate collapse and obliteration of the Japanese nation, but also it would lead to the total extinction of human civilization."

Following the victory of the allies following World War II and the United States' occupation of Japan, with the need to rebuild, loyalty to the state moved to loyalty to the economy.

Against this backdrop, Taiichi Ohno began to work at Toyota in Japan. Initially supervising the floor of an engine manufacturing shop in the plant, he eventually worked his way up to being an executive.

Between 1948 and 1975, Taiichi Ohno and Eiji Toyoda developed the Toyota Production System (TPS). This was the foundation of LEAN manufacturing and the "just-in-time" approach.

This manufacturing system spread across the world, to the United States and beyond. With Brexit on the agenda, many people in the UK heard of the risks of disruption affecting the just-in-time supply chain.

But what does this actually mean?

The principals are lengthy and many people often spend much of their lives trying to understand these systems. But having already had to learn all of this over many years, let me explain it in as brief terms as possible.

A former mentor of mine described how he learnt this process whilst working for Honda in Japan. As they explained it:

Imagine a lion chasing a dazzle of zebras. The lion sets its sight on a single zebra as its prey and catches it. If the lion was to constantly switch its target, it would go home hungry.

In many engineering teams, there is so much work going on at once, but nothing is ever completed. This is known as "work-in-progress", or WIP. LEAN manufacturing limits the amount of WIP, trying to instead get more work actually completed.

In manufacturing, the way this is done is through a process of continuous improvement which is followed until the batch sizes keep being lowered more and more.

In poorly-managed engineering teams, new work will be started before old work is completed. Then all work will ultimately accumulate into a bottleneck and not actually deliver business value. Expensive product is being worked on but it's not in a position to be sold. It just accumulates space and costs money.

Instead, by identifying and removing the bottlenecks, batch sizes can be reduced. When batch sizes are reduced, work flows quicker, meaning issues in quality and speed can be addressed and the business can react faster to market needs.

This is the secret to the Toyota Production System.

Another improvement paradigm is the theory of constraints, produced by Eliyahu Goldratt and based on the Toyota Production System. In his book, *The Goal*, Goldratt presents a process of transforming a low performing manufacturing plant into a high performing one through following a continuous process of removing bottlenecks in order to improve flow in a system.

The first step is to identify the constraint. Then there follows a process to be able to address the constraint so it's no longer a limiting factor. The process is then repeated with the next constraint.

The system focusses on global efficiency, not just making people do as much work as possible for the sake of local efficiencies.

As Goldratt said: "Activating a non-bottleneck to its maximum is an act of maximum stupidity."

This may sound obvious, but it's hugely profound and a lesson that many still don't understand.

I recently read a report about an insolvent technology company. The company was bought by a new investor, who discovered during the due diligence phase that the company was in a concerning position. Having spent over £100,000 in legal fees, the investor decided to buy the business for £1. He was unaware that large amounts of staff were being laid off and clients were complaining.

Whilst the new owner decided to shut down one of the worst performing parts of the business, which was developing software for clients, he later discovered that over 120 clients had paid for work they hadn't yet received. The new owner had no option but to sub-contract the work to other suppliers and former employees.

At the same time, the loss-making nature of the business warranted deeper cuts – meaning the company had no new business coming in as there were no longer any salespeople. Salespeople who moved on were offering the same services as the business but at a cheaper rate.

The UK tax office (HMRC) wasn't willing to wait for the debt any longer and was petitioning for the business to be shut down. Eventually the assets of the company were sold to a new entity and the company was written off with over £6,100,000 owed to creditors.

Reducing work-in-progress can clearly help resolve disasters, but the journey here goes further. In February 2021, a group of 17 software development practitioners wrote

the Agile Manifesto. The manifesto goes like
this:

> *We are uncovering better ways of
> developing software by doing it and
> helping others do it.*
>
> *Through this work we have come to
> value:*
>
> *Individuals and interactions over
> processes and tools*
>
> *Working software over comprehensive
> documentation*
>
> *Customer collaboration over contract
> negotiation*
>
> *Responding to change over following a
> plan*
>
> *That is, while there is value in the items
> on the right, we value the items on the left
> more.*

This manifesto was adopted into various
methodologies, initially rapid application
development (RAD), but later methodologies

called Scrum, extreme programming and Kanban.

The 2020 Standish CHAOS Report details that whilst just 13% of projects using the traditional waterfall methodology succeed (meaning delivered on time, on budget and with required features and functions), this increases to 42% for projects using an Agile methodology.

So far so good?

However, this is where things start to get tricky. I conducted research for the company Haystack and found that around 70% of software projects fail to be delivered on-time. Prior research also found that this was the case despite 83% of software engineers rating the importance of on-time completion as high or very high.

With the help of the research agency J.L. Partners I conducted research among 500 business decision-makers in the US and the UK. We found that 81% in the UK and 89% in the US are concerned about on-time delivery of software projects in their organisations. Of these, 44% in the UK and 57% in the US said they were "very concerned".

The Agile approach works to address late software delivery by making the process go faster. However, this is not the solution.

Let's first start with project estimates that require projects to be delivered by a certain deadline. One potential reason for this is those who over-promise and underdeliver. Prior research shows that "those with the lowest programming skill" are most likely to be over-optimistic at estimating delivery in large projects.

Inflated self-assessment of performance is not uncommon in software engineering, where 2023 research I conducted with Survation found 94% of software engineers rate their job performance as average or above. Men are 26% more likely than women to consider themselves better than average performers.

The results from a historical study were consistent with this, finding that software engineers tend to overestimate their performance by up to 42%, rating themselves in the top 5%.

In addition to software engineers being overly optimistic with delivery estimates, another reason for late delivery is unrealistic commercial demands from management.

The teachings of Agile, like reducing the amount of work-in-progress and reducing task switching, are hugely powerful in improving software delivery. However, in many environments Agile is then simply used as an excuse to get developers to work faster and harder, leading to the neglect of engineering rigour and heightening the risk of potentially fatal outcomes.

Recall the Toyota unintended acceleration bug at the start of this book. In his professional evidence during the trial, Michael Barr of the Barr Group pointed to internal communication within Toyota, stating: "In truth, technology such as failsafe is not part of the Toyota Engineering division's DNA".

The Post Office's Horizon IT project was one of the first IT projects in the world to use Agile – specifically rapid application development (RAD).

The lack of concrete requirements through the use of RAD has become a recurring theme in the evidence heard by the Horizon IT Inquiry. Before the inquiry, Terence Austin, a Fujitsu project director, remarked: "one of the reasons why this got into this situation is that we were forced to do rapid application development and, by doing that, you haven't got a functional specification".

David McDonnell said in his evidence to the Horizon IT Inquiry:

> *Well, a project such as that—well, any kind of software development project—there should be a framework of how the team work. It should start with the design documents. That's the target of what you*

*are trying to deliver; that's what you are building against.*

*... I know that there had been some documents that were reverse engineered, but they were irrelevant and out of date, and they weren't even in the building when I got there. I had to ask for them.*

In 2009, the CEO of Facebook (now Meta), Mark Zuckerberg had said: "Unless you are breaking stuff, you are not moving fast enough." This was consistent with the company's internal motto until 2014: "Move fast and break things".

This trend appears to be changing, however. Recall how earlier in the book we discussed how the wind was changing towards the public favouring safe and secure computer systems over those which just provide the latest features as quickly as possible.

Agility often comes at the cost of predictability, making it hard to estimate when functionality will be delivered, however it seems that many software teams wish to change the balance towards predictability.

The polling of business leaders seems to corroborate that quality plays an important role. In reaction to the statement "The goal of a software engineering team is to deliver high-quality software on time", 98% in the UK and 96% in the US agreed, with 65% in the UK and 62% in the US strongly agreeing.

In the next chapter, we'll discuss how the desire to move fast has led to disastrous outcomes.

# Burnout

In 2021, with Survation, I conducted research that found 83% of software engineers were suffering from work-related burnout to various extents. By 2023, this benchmark hadn't shifted, with 81% still reporting symptoms of burnout to some extent.

In both these periods, more than half of software engineers polled would say the level of burnout they faced was either moderate or high.

In the 2021 research, I also studied why this was the case. In the first instance we asked questions related to pandemic-related causes of burnout, however "increased workload" came top of 12 different dimensions.

I then tried asking about 10 dimensions related to general reasons. Still, "high workload" came top with 47% reporting this as a reason for their burnout.

Software engineering can be a tough, exhausting career. Complex and brittle technology combined with a high psychological workload can easily take their toll. However, over recent years further practices have increased the levels of burnout amongst software engineers.

We've previously covered how 70% of software projects fail to be delivered on-time. As a result, in the name of Agile, shortcuts are often taken and the team is pushed to work harder to meet their deadlines.

In many cases, the central teaching from Agile of reducing work-in-progress is lost and many teams are treated as working in an Agile way just because they follow some of the ritualistic practises of the methodology. For example, teams will work in two-week "sprints" and have daily "stand-up" meetings, despite there being vast amounts of work-in-progress.

As a result, the pressure to work ever harder continues to mount. In this context, software engineers are pushed to work ever faster, often with technical risks being neglected and greater levels of burnout developing.

Nowadays, there are a plethora of engineering management tools and performance metrics frameworks which will push engineers to ship out work ever faster, even in the face of unmitigated risk.

One such metrics framework that was recently popular was the so-called DORA four key metrics – named after a team which was acquired by Google.

The metrics framework would evaluate software delivery performance purely through the metric of speed. Two of the headline metrics included the speed to deploy software and the frequency at which software was deployed. Even the metrics for reliability were rooted in the time to resolve issues (rather than the number, severity or risk of issues), and the percentage of deployments that would fail.

These metrics would later become abused to monitor the performance of software engineers.

When humans are put under stress, like during burnout, a hormone called cortisol surges in our bodies. Having too high levels of cortisol in your body can lead to a variety of ill effects – from weight gain and poor sleep, to anxiety and high blood pressure. There is even evidence that persistent stress can lead to vision loss.

This stress inevitably has an impact on the ability to deliver software on-time, from high staff turnover to decreased performance.

The solution is to address the problems which cause businesses to not be able to commit to delivery against realistic timelines.

Rather than simply getting software engineers to work faster, it's important to address the desire of businesses to be able to commit to work based on informed delivery timescales, without the appearance of unmitigated risks which affect on-time delivery of software.

By making sure the requirements of new projects are clear and ensuring deadlines are agreed and communicated with software engineers, we are able to find immediate solutions to the need for predictability whilst addressing the problem of developer burnout.

# Psychological Safety

Therac-25 was a computer-controlled radiation therapy device produced by a Canadian company, AECL. Eleven machines were installed in the US and Canada.

In two years between 1985 and 1987 a total of six patients received massive radiation overdoses, with three of them dying as a result. The injuries for those who survived included disability and scarring for one patient, a total hip replacement needed for another and a third requiring breast removal and loss of the use of an arm.

We know little of the system itself as AECL claims intellectual property rights over the software design. However, we do know that the software was written by a single software engineer over a period of several years. This engineer left his position at AECL in 1986 and his name is not publicly known. Likewise, we don't know his professional background or experience.

There were clear errors in the software engineering of the device. When the US Food and Drug Administration investigated the device, a reviewer said: "Unfortunately, the AECL response also seems to point out an apparent lack of documentation on software specifications and a software test plan."

This is a common issue in software catastrophes. In well-engineered systems there is a specification that links the customer's requirements to the technical design of the system.

According to a paper by Professor Sara Baase, when concerns were raised, AECL assured machine operators that overdoses were impossible.

According to a paper by Dr Nancy Levenson, despite many hardwired safety systems moved to the software in the new model, AECL was convinced the Therac-25 software was free of bugs.

Throughout this book, we've seen many examples where when catastrophic failures emerge, systems are defended as perfect. This is a symptom of a problem where there is a lack of psychological safety. In short, psychological safety is where people aren't subjected to detriment for speaking up with ideas, questions, concerns or mistakes.

In 1999, Dr Amy Edmondson was studying clinical teams and the number of mistakes they'd make. To her horror, Dr Edmonson noticed that the teams with better outcomes actually made more mistakes than teams with less good outcomes.

However, with further research, Dr Edmondson later found that this was due to teams with better outcomes admitting to more mistakes, whilst the less successful teams sought to conceal their mistakes.

This research entered the world of software engineering when Google's Project Aristotle team started researching what made some teams perform better. The researchers studied a total of 180 teams, including 115 project teams in engineering. In discussing the results of the research, Google said:

"Psychological safety was far and away the most important of the five dynamics we found".

Later industry-wide research conducted by Google verified this in 2018, finding "that this culture of psychological safety is predictive of software delivery performance, organizational performance, and productivity".

In their *Guidance on Risk*, Engineering Council UK say: "Engineering professionals should [...] encourage a culture of 'open reporting' and a spirit of questioning and learning from others [and] avoid a 'good news only' or closed culture".

Often poor engineering leaders will either believe that closed cultures are good or that it is possible to regulate such a psychologically safe culture into existence. The truth is that it's far deeper ingrained into the culture of an organisation.

In a 2004 paper in the British Medical Journal's *Quality & Safety* publication, Dr Ron

Westrum defined how different organisations process information. He did this by creating a typology which grouped organisations into three different cultures: pathological (power-oriented), bureaucratic (rule-oriented) and generative (performance oriented).

In pathological organisations, messengers are "shot", and responsibilities are shirked. Failure leads to scapegoating and novelty is crushed.

In bureaucratic organisations, messengers are neglected and there are narrow responsibilities. Failure leads to justice and novelty leads to problems.

In generative cultures, messengers are trained, and risks are shared. Failure leads to inquiry and novelty is implemented.

When faced with a problem, often managers find it easy to resort to introducing new rules, but this is not what helps an organisation nurture a generative culture. Regulation is needed in some cases, but the real challenge is building psychologically safe environments where people feel free to raise the alarm to issues when they first emerge.

Recall earlier in the book I introduced research on how 75% of software engineers faced retaliation the last time they reported wrongdoing. In this same study, I also asked software engineers whether they could take calculated risks without fear of negative consequences. Nearly one in four said they couldn't, while 17% also said they couldn't admit to mistakes and 15% said they couldn't express ideas and concerns or speak-up with questions.

Additionally, recall that a majority of software engineers who did not report wrongdoing when they encountered it cited fear of retaliation from management as a reason.

With a majority of software engineers (53%) having suspected unethical behaviour occurring at work during their careers, psychological safety is vital to them feeling able to raise the alarm when such issues come up.

The importance of this is underscored with the latest data showing that 92% of software engineers are concerned about software reliability at their workplace to some extent, with 34% "greatly concerned" and 38% "moderately concerned".

In this chapter we have identified what is missing for organisations to improve. In the next chapter I want to look at whether it's possible for such organisations to change.

# Turnaround?

As of 2024, many start-ups are currently zombies. They took too much capital and scaled too fast without knowing whether they have product-market fit or not. Now these organisations find themselves in a position where they count down the days they have to live, lurching from funding round to funding round, desperate to survive.

The UK government came along during the pandemic to back a number of these failing companies through its Future Fund. Under the scheme, the government would provide automatic loans to start-ups which had to be matched by the private sector. These loans would convert to equity at the next funding round.

Nearly £1.14 billion was ploughed into such companies. Pollen, the bankrupt business described earlier, was one such beneficiary.

With money issued through the government-owned British Business Bank, the bank warned the government it would only attract "second tier" firms that couldn't find funds from elsewhere.

In a June 2021 audit meeting, non-executive director Dharmash Mistry warned the start-ups backed would face a "limited chance of growth to a sufficient scale for success" resulting in some "zombie businesses".

More broadly, there are even more zombie companies in the private sector who have been backed with high levels of money or debt financing but will likely never grow into profitable businesses.

These zombies are upon us now.

To reach this position, those running these businesses must have ignored so much feedback from data, customers and investors, amongst others. Numerous opportunities to either fail fast or refuse to build something that would ultimately go wrong were missed. Whilst these companies could have attempted to pivot to a better area of business, they did not take the opportunity to do so successfully.

In many of the computer scandals we've covered in this book, from the Post Office Horizon IT system to Therac-25 radiation machines, signs of feedback were ignored.

I've spent a couple of years working as a transformation consultant, seeking to help turn businesses and technology teams around from the edge. There are few people who do this effectively and we form somewhat of a small community. Many of these individuals go from company-to-company performing such transformations.

This is not something which forms a substantial part of my consultancy practice currently; it is rarely worth undertaking unless there are serious hallmarks of a particular case having the potential for success.

Of all practitioners, the industry-wide success rate for "digital transformations" is around one in three. However, these are typically highly focussed technical transformations with executive sponsorship. Cultural transformations are far less likely and often require backing from very senior executives, if not the CEO.

Companies with good corporate governance will often hire a "transformation CEO" (a CEO who is highly experienced at conducting such transformations) to lead the efforts from the top-down. This CEO may use transformation consultancy services to help them.

In engineering teams, my experience is that managers can only seek to make improvements from the top-down in the areas they control.

However, what is to be said of managing up? Surely it's possible to convince leadership there is a brighter way forward?

That is the promise in the books *The Phoenix Project* and *The Unicorn Project*, both of which are IT transformation works based on the premise of the theory of constraints novel *The Goal* by Eliyahu Goldratt, which I discussed earlier.

However, the reality is that transformation projects are far from a guaranteed success. The only cases where I've seen the approach of bottom-up change find success is when the leader is willing to make a change. In most other cases, it won't work.

The promise of limitless growth potential with support is a nice ideal, but the psychological reality appears to be that people are far more constrained in their abilities to change unless they're willing to put in the effort to do so.

When a disaster is in motion, the way it is often stopped is by appropriate governance oversight taking steps to address the problem.

This is why governance is so essential for such organisations, why whistleblowers need the ability to raise the alarm and why, in appropriate cases, it's important to inform the employer of a person overruling professional advice and the risks that can result from this.

In other cases, internal whistleblowing champions, journalists and those who partake in external whistleblowing play an important role.

The model for why bottom-up transformations fail is complex but let me briefly summarise my current model to help explain why.

In many instances, transformations have been attempted before and failed. Those in positions of power have received constructive feedback from users, investors and employees, but it hasn't been taken onboard. This feedback could concern anything from culture, technology or product.

In my experience I've found that this particular issue seems to correlate with narcissism.

I won't speak in psychological terms as I'm not qualified to diagnose, however psychologists use the DSM-5 criteria to diagnose narcissistic personality disorder in instances where there are at least five of the following nine characteristics:

1. A grandiose sense of self-importance.
2. A preoccupation with fantasies of unlimited success, power, brilliance, beauty or ideal love.
3. A belief that they are special and unique and can only be understood by, or should associate with, other special or high-status people or institutions.
4. A need for excessive admiration.
5. A sense of entitlement.
6. Interpersonally exploitative behaviour.
7. A lack of empathy.
8. Envy of others or a belief that others are envious of them.
9. A demonstration of arrogant and haughty behaviours or attitudes.

In many cases, transformation consultants can find themselves drawn to these types of personalities due to an intrinsic need they feel to fix situations. This rarely goes well, unless the narcissist believes the successes are their own achievements.

Psychology shows that narcissistic abuse is horrible. Whilst it isn't persistent, when it's bad, it's bad. Victims can expect to be gaslighted (forced to question their own interpretation of reality), have blame shifted to themselves and have personal boundaries ignored. In such an environment, if you try to perform a transformation you can expect malicious gossiping, bullying and sabotage.

In these situations, for your own wellbeing and career, often the only way forward is to take away the power from the narcissist and cut off your relationship with them.

Dr Ramani Durvasula, an expert on the psychology of narcissism, says in response to whether narcissists can change: "… my read on the clinical evidence is no, not really."

Dr Ramani goes on to explain that the odds of change are even lower given narcissism is associated with poor reflective capacity.

Clearly not everyone in these situations is a narcissist. In other circumstances there can be a reluctance to accept the pain that comes with the need to make changes.

This concept is explained very well in Dr Anna Lembke's book *Dopamine Nation*. Essentially, whilst the brain is quite complex, the model argues that the brain attempts to keep a balance of both pain and pleasure. Too much pleasure not only dampens your ability to feel pleasure, but also reduces your tolerance to pain, Lembke argues.

Dr Robert H. Lustig goes further in his book *The Hacking of the American Mind*, where he separates the concepts of reward and contentment, stating: "Pleasure (reward) is the emotional state where your brain says, 'This feels good – I want more,' while happiness (contentment) is the emotional state where your brain says, 'This feels good – I don't want or need any more.'"

Dr Lustig goes on to say, "chronic excess reward interferes with contentment".

These ideas tie in with Prospect Theory, originated in a paper by the psychologists Daniel Kahneman and Amos Tversky in a paper entitled "Prospect Theory: An Analysis of Decision under Risk".

Backed by controlled studies, Prospect Theory posits that humans feel the pain of losses far greater than the pleasure of wins. For example, experiments indicated that the pain of losing $1,000 could only be compensated by the pleasure of winning $2,000.

Robert Prentice, a professor at The University of Texas at Austin, describes the relationship as follows: "Prospect theory describes how people tend to take much greater risks to avoid losing things compared to the risks they would've taken to gain those things in the first place. Sometimes, to avoid a loss, we consciously decide to lie. We cover up what might be a simple accidental mistake because we don't wish to suffer the consequences of making that mistake."

Many in tech dream of working in environments where there are snacks and cold brew coffee on tap, pumping dopamine-rich caffeine and sugar into our bloodstreams. Alongside this, they want the satisfaction of frequent reward without needing to produce something of meaningful worth, combined with the salary and benefits of working in big tech.

When I was early in my career, working in a traditional engineering environment in a window-less warehouse in middle England where I wouldn't eat the plain digestive biscuits out of fear of being added to the purchase rota, I would always wonder why people would leave more comfortable jobs in favour of doing something more difficult. Now I'm in the position where this is something I've done myself multiple times.

In truth, people in such jobs don't necessarily actually feel more intrinsically happy than anyone else. In some cases, their intrinsic need to do something of value in the world will be so great that they will leave those careers to work on something high-risk.

However, for some people, their baseline of pleasure will have increased so much that the potential risk of failing hurts too much.

Alongside this, one can imagine that some people who live in luxury city-centre flats and have the latest electric vehicle, children in private school and a partner with expensive tastes will struggle to take risks or rock the boat.

Ironically, this risk sensitivity can make the risk of failure far greater.

This serves as a reminder of the importance of seeking things which make us intrinsically happy over materialistic outcomes.

Sometimes transformations do work, but this is often only in a limited area where you have direct control. Ultimately the survival of this work is then at the mercy of the health of a global system.

If a transformation is what you want to
attempt – something I've successfully done
many times – by all means, go for it. But be
very cautious of the risks.

# Resilience

It was the 7th of October 2008, and Qantas Flight 72 – regarded as the "world's safest airline" – was leaving Singapore's Changi Airport enroute to Perth Airport in Western Australia.

As a frequent passenger of Singapore Changi Airport, the luxury surroundings certainly do a great job of relaxing you before your flight. The amenities include an indoor pool, a butterfly garden, a movie theatre, a food court and, since 2019, even an indoor waterfall you can ride past on a shuttle train.

The flight would take place on an Airbus A330-303. The first variant of the Airbus A330 range first took flight in 1992. This particular plane was nearly five years old, having been delivered new to Qantas in November 2003. The type of engines used was changed in November 2004.

The flight crew was led by Captain Kevin Sullivan, with First Officer Peter Lipsett and Second Officer Ross Hales. There were an additional nine cabin crew in the plane. The flight was carrying 303 passengers, for a total of 315 people onboard the flight.

Captain Sullivan was a former pilot in the US Navy who had moved to Australia. First Officer Lipsett was also from a navy background, except in his case with the Royal Australian Navy. The young second officer was in flight to allow the captain and second officer to be able to rest during flight, as the complete roundtrip time from Perth and back would typically be over 10 hours.

This would be just their second time flying together, the first being the flight there the previous night.

The packed flight took off without issue, but soon after take-off the "master caution" warning light had illuminated. The team began to debug the problem, first with Captain Sullivan turning on the autopilot to give himself space to think and First Officer Lipsett turning off the warning so as to not distract them (per standard procedure).

Gone are the days of aircraft being simplistic mechanical constructions. Instead, computers have taken the place of flight engineers who used to station themselves in the cockpit.

Whilst the amount of computer code in an Airbus A330 isn't readily known, the Boeing 787 Dreamliner is powered by seven million lines of code.

Recall how Toyota's cars were written in the C programming language (with many manufacturers complying with the MISRA-C rules to ensure the system is reliable), however planes and defence systems like nuclear-armed submarines are built slightly differently. Instead, they are programmed in a language called Ada. Ada is named after Ada Lovelace, a 19th century British countess who is often credited with being the first computer programmer and the first person to recognise that machines could do more than just mere calculations.

The Ada language was designed in the 1970s by the United States Department of Defence to meet the requirements of the British Ministry of Defence and their own.

One feature of Ada is that it can be mathematically checked, by telling the computer what is meant to go into a small piece of code (preconditions), come out (postconditions) and what should not change (invariants), alongside using tightly defined definitions of what the moving variables in the code do. It is then possible to mathematically prove that much of the code is correct. This is known as "formal verification" and is supported in the SPARK dialect of the Ada language.

This approach has been so robust that when Altran UK built a system called Tokeneer for the United States' National Security Agency, they used a robust engineering process and encouraged academics to try and find defects in the approximately 10,000 lines of code. The process would work by using a strong requirements engineering process, which would cascade down into mathematically verified code. Despite rigorous testing, only four minor defects which don't affect functionality have been found so far.

It's unclear to what extent such verification was done on the Airbus A330, but in 2011, AdaCore reported that the aerial refuelling system of a military model of the Airbus A330 had undergone this verification. The model concerned, the Airbus A330 MRTT, is currently in use by a number of militaries around the world and even serves as the UK government's VIP plane – used by government ministers like the prime minister and the royal family.

Nowadays, Toyota have been reported to be doing work using the Ada SPARK language, perhaps unsurprisingly given the software issues we explored in the introduction of this book.

This aircraft software also runs on real-time operating systems. Unlike the operating system your home computer would use, a physical clock is used to ensure data is processed within tight time constraints.

Returning to our flight, the flight computer indicated to the pilots that the issue was to do with the system that takes air from the engines in order to pressurise the cabin. The advanced computer also displayed a set of instructions to diagnose the issue. The first officer carried out these steps whilst the captain monitored the flight, turning the plane to avoid a thunderstorm ahead.

The plane was flying in clear skies and the issue was resolved without the passengers even knowing.

Soon the second officer would take over next to the captain as the first officer went to rest. This was to ensure there were three fully-rested pilots in the cockpit during the most dangerous parts of the flight: take-off and landing.

However, the issues in this flight would appear mid-flight.

Suddenly the autopilot disengaged, and the captain took manual control of the flight until the secondary autopilot was engaged.

This time it wasn't the amber "master warning" light that was lit, but the red "master caution" that illuminated. The computer was riddled with error messages appearing and soon after a robotic voice started repeating the warning "stall".

Physicists still don't have one theory to explain why planes stay in the air, however if the plane is too slow or the nose of the plane is too high, it can stall and fall from the sky. Naturally, this is considered an urgent warning. However, the instruments in the cockpit were also indicating that the plane was going too fast – over speeding. Clearly both could not happen at once.

At least the back-up instruments and the instincts of the first officer were correct, meaning the flight could be flown using this information.

What the pilots didn't know at the time is they were encountering a rare computer issue. The Airbus A330 is equipped with three devices called Air Data Inertial Reference

Units (ADIRUs). These were manufactured by Northrop Grumman, an American company.

ADIRUs contain a computer and use a variety of sensors including a laser gyroscope to provide fault-tolerant data about the aircraft. Three are in use for safety, at least that's the theory. Two of these ADIRUs serve as the primary ones and one is designated as a secondary.

If the data of the angle of the plane is consistent and accurate, the A330's main computer will simply take the average of the result from both primary ADIRUs and use that. However, if one of the two primary ADIRU units deviated from the result of the other primary ADIRU and the backup ADIRU, a stored result is used for the next 1.2 seconds.

The limitation is that if the 1.2 second period ended and coincided with another inaccurate reading, the computer software was not designed to deal with that eventuality.

Whilst certainty a rare failure, this is something which could arise from a hardware weakness combined with environmental conditions. (Consider how, in the Toyota case, Barr's testimony was that a single cosmic ray causing a single "0" to flip to a "1" or vice-versa could cause unintended acceleration.)

The captain told the second officer to call the first officer back to the flight deck and began flying the plane manually, as the autopilot didn't have the information to fly itself. The second officer attempted to silence the alarms, but they kept sounding.

Previously the plane was flying 5 degrees over the horizon, but suddenly it lurched downwards to -45 degrees and sped up. The captain, held in his seat only by his lap belt, was desperately trying to pull the plane's nose back.

Those in the cabin who were unrestrained (and even some who were) found themselves thrown across the cabin. Some would be pinned to the ceiling, even becoming sandwiched between the ceiling and pieces of luggage, which crashed into them.

Even after the captain released the controls, nothing happened and the pilots could see the blue of the Indian Ocean they were to crash into should they not be able to stop it.

In aircraft, sometimes computers can follow their own instructions instead of the pilots'. The computer, calculating from the data that a stall was imminent, acted to stop a dangerous pilot from crashing the plane. However, this calculation was wrong.

Captain Sullivan had another trick up his sleeve. Slowly and iteratively pulling the control stick, he was able to raise the nose. Knowing passengers would be stuck to the ceiling, he was careful to avoid pulling the nose up too fast.

The captain advised the cabin to strap themselves in, then put on his shoulder harnesses as they looked for the issue. Whilst some people respond in non-productive ways or become frozen during engineering incidents, the pilots here were displaying incredible levels of focus and calm despite the adrenaline they were certainly experiencing.

The computer suggested that one of the inflight computers, known as PRIM3, should be reset.

There are five computers known as Flight Control Data Concentrators (FCDCs). They are known as PRIM1, PRIM2, PRIM3, SEC1 and SEC2. At any one time, only one can be the primary computer, which then processes orders and sends them to the other computers.

In the event PRIM1 cannot be the primary computer (for example, if there's an error or it's switched off), PRIM2 takes over. In the event both are unavailable, PRIM3 will take over.

In the event all the PRIM computers are disabled, the SEC1 or SEC2 computers can fly the plane themselves. When this mode is enabled, there is no autopilot, and the flight computer will treat the pilot's instructions as gospel – whatever they instruct will directly be matched into action. This is known as "direct law". Where needed, the plane can automatically switch between "normal law", "alternative law 1", "alternative law 2", "direct law" and in the worst-case scenario there's a mechanical backup where no protections are available. These changes happen automatically, and a pilot is not expected to start pulling circuit breakers or switching off systems in order to change the flight laws.

After consulting the captain's copy of the paper operating manual (the second officer's was thrown across the cockpit), the second officer lifted the guard covering a switch and reset the computer. The warnings then disappeared.

However, shortly after the problem reoccurred, causing the plane to drop again. Again, pulling the nose up slowly was successful.

As he did the last time this happened, Captain Sullivan coached the second officer to take deep breaths in order to manage his stress. The errors would reappear on the computer and as the second officer worked through the issues, he noticed that the PRIM3 computer was reporting another fault, suggesting that it be reset.

Remembering the second dive, they decided they wouldn't try resetting the computer a second time. The captain made an announcement telling the passengers to make sure they had their seatbelts fastened. The second officer asked the cabin crew to bring the first officer back to the flight deck.

Since the second dive, the captain had noticed that one of the automations designed to keep the plane level when there are no inputs was no longer working. This led him to believe the plane was now operating in "direct law" mode. However, the warning message about this safety feature being disabled that should ordinarily appear when the plane is in "direct law" never appeared. Would the problem therefore reoccur?

Warnings eerily appeared and disappeared on the computer screen. The second officer attempted to press the emergency cancel button to suppress them multiple times, but the warnings continued.

The first officer returned after being granted entry to the cockpit, taking his seat beside the captain from the second officer.

With the computers at risk of causing another dive at any moment, they agreed to get the plane on the ground as quickly as they could – diverting to a nearby military airfield.

The first officer wanted to declare the most serious emergency – a mayday. The captain, however, decided to declare a "pan", which is the second most serious. The captain didn't yet know what had happened in the cabin.

They would be landing in an unknown airport. The flight computer had stopped responding when they tried to input the airport they would be flying to, meaning they would have to navigate an unfamiliar airport by eye and under stress.

The flight attendants, including an off-duty Qantas employee called Diana Casey, were trying to help passengers. Casey answered a call from the cockpit using the intercom and reported the scale of injuries in the cabin. There were bone fractures, lacerations, spinal injuries and even passengers still hanging from the ceiling after crashing into it during the dives.

This is when Captain Sullivan changed his mind in response to new information and decided to declare a mayday. This would cause a nationwide alert, with emergency response services descending on the airfield they were planning to land in.

The pilots felt their ears popping and noticed the automatic system for controlling cabin pressure had also failed, meaning they would need to adjust this manually.

The failure of the automations meant they had a plethora of tasks which would ordinarily be designated to automate. The list of systems that weren't working was too long to name during the attempted landing. At the same time, they were trying to diagnose the issues and contact an operations centre in Sydney via a satellite phone to see what data they were receiving about the plane.

The pilots worked through their enormous workload, with Captain Sullivan telling the occasional joke to keep morale up.

After carefully testing the plane's controllability, they decided they would land the plane defensively in the event it entered another dive. Control was good, but during the final descent, the stall warning sounded again.

In the cabin, some passengers were praying and others were crying as they saw how close to the ground they were.

Captain Sullivan had devised a plan in case the plane did attempt to dive again. By coming in at speed, the controls would be more responsive if the plane did enter a dive. Second, he had a backup plan which would use the rudders instead of the sidestick to lift the plane. This risky manoeuvre would involve turning the plane to its side and stomping on the rudder.

Recall that the warning message about an automation being disabled did not appear on the computer as it should have when the plane was in "direct law" mode, which would have disabled the automation at fault.

However, the plane was not in "normal mode", either. It turns out there was another software issue at hand. When the plane was in one of the "alternative law" modes, the plane computer wasn't designed to display this message despite the automation being off. This issue would later be rectified by Airbus in a future software update.

Fortunately, both the "alternative law" modes disabled the automation which was at issue.

They successfully manually landed the plane. Of the 315 passengers onboard, 118 had been injured, and 12 of these were serious injuries. However, everyone survived.

In the remote airfield, the few emergency services available worked for hours to rescue those with the most severe injuries.

The psychological safety within the air transportation industry meant that a forensic investigation into the computers could be conducted, identifying the issue in a report by the Australian Transportation Safety Board.

This psychological safety that has traditionally existed in the aviation industry has been put to the test recently with crises affecting Boeing, including software issues on the Boeing 737 Max aircraft, bolts missing from the door of another 737 Max aircraft and a Boeing whistleblower being found dead in an apparent suicide in 2024. In response, in March 2024, three top Boeing executives including the CEO announced they would step down.

Nevertheless, in the days after the incident described here, Airbus was able to publish emergency guidance to pilots who faced the same warnings, by turning the ADIRU 1 off.

This incident did repeat in the months that followed and the advice helped prevent the issue reoccurring.

However, in another Qantas flight the issue re-emerged despite the crew following the steps.

It turned out that the ADIRU was not turned off because of another issue, so further emergency guidance was issued on how to de-energise the ADIRU in this situation.

In both Qantas Flight 72 and the subsequent flight, a failure in the ADIRUs was never found (although the faulty data from the computers was evident in the forensic investigations).

According to *AeroTime Hub*, Airbus also issued a software update to prevent the bug where erroneous data 1.2 seconds apart is received from recurring.

In this situation, the computers failed but no one died. At its core, it's what a friend of mine, Piet van Dongen, often discusses at software conferences: resilience engineering.

Software engineers often can protect against potential failures which are known through engineering systems to be more robust.

Nevertheless there are what Piet refers to as "unknown unknowns" – risks which are fundamentally surprising to engineers. These unknown unknowns are things we both are unaware of and have little knowledge to rectify.

In an operating theatre, when an unknown unknown occurs, the medical team are there to address the problems and care for the patients.

During Qantas Flight 72, the team of pilots were able to rapidly respond to the issues while under immense pressure through hard work, strong communication and psychological safety.

Almost every service you use, from social media to the power grid, is backed by teams of on-call engineers who are working around the clock, ready to intervene when systems fail. In other words, they formed a socio-technical system to address the issues.

In many of the examples we've explored throughout this book, when unknown unknowns did emerge, those involved did not act to inquire into the failures. This led to these failures not being addressed and resulting catastrophic outcomes.

During ongoing incidents and the remediation phases, humans are ultimately part of the system. It is key that we can therefore respond under pressure to address things when they go wrong.

Netflix is one company that uses "chaos engineering" to test how resilient systems are. Using a robot called "chaos monkey", parts of their computer systems will be disrupted to see how teams respond.

However, it is worth noting that this is a technical tool and isn't a silver bullet to addressing the human parts of a system, which are often neglected in failures.

The Engineering Council UK's *Guidance on Risk* I referred to earlier instructs engineers to "ensure that human factors are considered" and to "look beyond purely technical considerations, to address non-technical factors, including social, economic, environmental and political perspectives".

As AI develops, it's therefore important that we use our brains when we encounter unmitigated risk and ensure people feel safe to raise the alarm to issues that emerge.

It goes beyond engineering, and we can all be part of this.

# Conclusion

Throughout this book, we've explored a number of catastrophic computer failures. In the last chapter, we saw how a courageous team defied the odds to battle a rogue computer that seemed intent on killing them. However, thankfully that issue was ultimately mitigated before it killed.

In the cases where computers have been able to kill, the technical reasons are different each time, but we see a combination of factors at play which are consistent in all cases.

Far from these factors being technical factors, they ultimately come down to human elements in the socio-technical system that surrounds how these systems are engineered.

First, there is an unquestioning belief in the reliability of the computer. Despite the fact that computers can be corrupted, sufficient steps are not taken to mitigate the potential risk due to the position of trust that we place in these computers. From allowing computers to overrule the instructions of a pilot and controlling the accelerator and brake on a vehicle, right through to determining the guilt of someone who was previously of good character, computers were put in positions of trust without the appropriate safeguards.

Computers are capable of a remarkable number of things and can do so with great accuracy, depending on how they're programmed. However, for them to occupy these positions of trust there must be lasting systems of oversight and scrutiny to ensure they are built in a way where they operate as expected. From designing a system and ensuring the requirements engineering process is done correctly, through to monitoring the system when it is in use.

As we interact with AI, we need to be conscious of the level of trust we choose to put into computers and be careful to not take them for granted. The same advice is true in helping protect ourselves from advanced cyberattacks.

Likewise, when you're asked to make a decision using computer information, especially when the decision is risky, it can often be useful to look at an audit log to check if the data is correct.

Second, every computer, even when programmed well, will ultimately encounter failure scenarios. These failures may well be "unknown unknowns" where we are unaware of the problems and have little knowledge to rectify them.

This is where we need to consider the broader system around a computer. Not just the technical system but the entire socio-technical system around it.

This is why, when many computer systems fail, there are robust teams who are there to respond and are trained to deal with such scenarios – from operations engineers who keep our online services alive to pilots who fly planes.

Key to these systems being effective is ensuring that people are able to raise the alarm when things look like they might be going wrong and that these people feel their advice will be listened to and taken onboard.

When people don't feel psychologically safe to raise suggestions, failures will be brushed under the carpet, only to come back with force later.

Unfortunately, the case studies in this book and the empirical research conducted indicates that this psychological safety is often lacking in software engineering teams, with many facing retaliation for reporting issues.

At the very least, people like David McDonnell, the former Fujitsu engineering manager, can enjoy a clearer conscience than those who did not speak up about such issues when they encountered them.

The engineering profession will benefit by aligning incentives engineers have for their own careers with those of society, to ensure they are suitably protected when they need to raise the alarm about serious issues.

In many cases we have also seen systems rushed to completion without the necessary safety engineering work being completed.

Frankly, proper business discipline is essential to ensuring that we never need to cut corners to get computer software out the door. Where it happens frequently, this is a sign of corporate mismanagement. This is especially the case in a culture where public appetite has become increasingly focussed on the stability of computer systems over getting the latest technology as quickly as possible.

As we see this broader shift in technology take root, there is rightfully an expectation that the public have technology that can be depended on. As technology becomes closely embedded in society, businesses and engineers must ensure these needs are met.

We have also seen cases where, when feedback is given, those in positions of control have not been receptive to criticism – often lashing out at others.

Proper systems of oversight and scrutiny are required to ensure that we do not have leaders who are insecure to the extent that this becomes a problem, and make sure that they are themselves able to resolve issues instead of choosing to bury their heads in the sand.

Killer computers emerge from toxic cultures, so ensuring we have healthy organisations where risk can be appropriately identified and managed is vital.

Finally, one of the primary aims of this book was to give advice to the public on how to avoid becoming victims to killer computers, so I wish to end with some direct advice to this point.

First, we have already covered the need to avoid having an unquestioning belief in the reliability of computers. Healthy scepticism has its advantages.

Whether it's AI showing us a highly convincing but untrue advertisement, an inaccurate calculation or even a scammer who has drafted an incredibly convincing phishing email, we need to keep our eyes peeled.

Second, utilise this healthy criticism to ensure that when things go wrong you intervene early to address the issues.

Like what we saw with Qantas Flight 72, sometimes you as the human need to be the safety check for a computer system that gets things wrong. Unfortunately, we didn't see this materialise in the Post Office scandal and apparently not in the current TV Licensing prosecutions either.

Be prepared to be part of the system rather than just an observer of it.

Third, be wary of the psychological phenomenon known as "commitment escalation" or "entrapment". In this phenomenon, being coerced to do something innocuous but wrong can lead to eventually being pressured to do something which is far worse.

Alan Bates resisted extreme pressure to sign-off faulty accounts. By refusing, he avoided the eventual criminal prosecution and ruin that many others faced.

Holding strong ethical principles from the start provides a robust defence against slowly being drawn into a pattern of eventually being part of something much worse. If we do find ourselves coerced into such a situation, it is important to always be prepared to draw the line and opt-out when our limits have been met.

At the time of writing, Apple recently launched their Vision Pro headset and the internet is ablaze with early adopters maximising the amount of simple pleasure they get from having the device strapped to their heads: from someone being stopped by police for driving whilst wearing the headset, to people using the device to consume entertainment whilst travelling on public transport.

The offices of tech companies have kitchens loaded with snacks and drinks filled with caffeine and sugar, which, like technology, trigger dopamine levels in our brain.

At the same time, the public have been subject to further technology issues. In March 2024, the British public was also impacted when software problems left a number of High Street takeaways and shops (Greggs, Sainsbury's, Tesco and McDonald's) unable to take payments. It remains unclear who or what is responsible for these outages. A high street bank, Nationwide Building Society, also faced an outage affecting purchases and payments.

Amongst these outages, there is one that is so far previously unreported. On the 20th of March 2024, London police officers took to social media after the Metropolitan Police's Connect IT system "imploded", reporting chaos in custody suites in the capital alongside an inability to begin applications for search warrants.

In August 2023, Computer Weekly had reported that the cost of the outsourced system was estimated to reach £214 million, this being £64 million overbudget. The system was designed to provide "end-to-end management of various policing processes, from intelligence and investigations to custody and prosecution".

Despite being a software engineer and computer scientist, having built my career on building the latest technology, I have never felt so grateful for my relatively technologically quiet life in Scotland. I may be writing this book on a laptop with a 14-inch screen and my broadband might not be as fast as in my old flat in London, but I am happier without those things for now.

Simpler activities like walking by the sea or talking to those who I love seem far more intrinsically satisfying than the immediate pleasure or stress that come from a life purely focussed on technology.

I feel it is important for us not to lose sight of this as we become ever more technologically advanced.

But don't get me wrong, it is hugely flattering for an engineer to see the impact they have made on the world.

Recently, after phoning my mobile phone network provider, they offered to sell me the ability to find out if my password was in a data breach as part of their cyber security offering for £2 a month. This was a technology I invented (but I didn't tell the call handler that).

Soon after I logged onto a social networking site to see a former colleague discussing some research I'd pioneered a few years ago, claiming that it supported an unrelated conclusion that subsequent research I did years later diverged from (but decided it wasn't the right moment to comment).

Whilst this all amused me, it nevertheless reminded me of how technology will be used in ways the inventor could never foresee – highlighting the importance of mitigating its risks.

Risk is inherent in new technology; it is essential that we take risks to advance as a species. But at the same time, we need to ensure these risks are well managed, alongside fostering an open and transparent culture that allows the discussion of such risks.

Humans play a critical role in managing the risks of new technology, as such, it's important we never forget about humans when we build new technology or imagine how it may evolve.

In short: No risk, no reward.

**THE END**